OFFICIAL GUIDE TO THE SMITHSONIAN

Smithsonian Institution Press
Washington, D.C.

Library of Congress Cataloging
in Publication Data

Smithsonian Institution.
Official guide to the Smithsonian.
Supt. of Docs. no.: SI 1.20 : Sm 5
1. Smithsonian Institution—Guide-books.
I. Title.
Q11.S79 1986 069'.09753 86-600282
ISBN 0-87474-711-2

First edition 1973; revised 1976, 1981, and
1986

10 9 8 7 6 5 4 3 2

Guidebook Staff
Hope Pantell, *Editor*
Maureen R. Jacoby, *Managing Editor*
Lisa Buck, *Designer*
Kathleen Brown, *Production Manager*

The following are among the many individuals who provided invaluable assistance in the preparation of this edition: Audrey Archer, Kathy Bartfield, Joanne Battista, Margaret Bertin, Susan Bliss, B. J. Bradley, Margery Byers, Rita Cipalla, Teri Davis, Mary Dyer, James Goode, Thomas Harney, Maria Heasly, Jeanie Kim, Joyce Lancaster, Linda McKnight, Michael Morgan, Mary Grace Potter, Michele Raphoon, Kathy Stafford, Ruth Selig, Michelle Smith, Linda St. Thomas, Sandra Westin

Building illustrations by Kate Howe Levy

Photo Credits: Ilene Berg Ackerman, Jack Buxbaum, Chris Capilongo, Chip Clark, Jessie Cohen, Al Harrell, E. Herter, Robert Lautman, Delmar Lipp, Eric Long, Eugene Mantie, Lillian M. O'Connell, Kim Nielsen, Dane Penland, Lee Stalsworth, Barbara K. Strong, John Tennant, Jeff Tinsley, Liz Zerbe, Smithsonian Institution Staff Photographers

CONTENTS

WELCOME
TO THE
SMITHSONIAN

When you visit the Smithsonian you will discover an institution that is unique in all the world. It is not, as many visitors imagine at first, simply a museum, or even a cluster of monumental museum buildings on the Mall in Washington, D.C. Rather, the Smithsonian is a national research and educational center, a vast intellectual network that encompasses—in addition to its exhibition halls and art galleries—laboratories, observatories, field stations, scientific expeditions, classrooms, advanced study groups, performing arts, publications, and much more. It belongs, in all its glorious diversity, to the people of the United States.

Founded with a mandate to add to the world's store of knowledge and to communicate that knowledge broadly, the Smithsonian Institution pursues this commitment in both scholarly and popular ways, one of them being the public display of objects from its wide-ranging collections. This book primarily concerns those objects on display, describing what is to be found in our 14 museums and telling how to go about locating the exhibits that are of special interest to each one of you. Historical treasures, significant scientific specimens, magnificent works of art—all are at the Smithsonian for your enjoyment and study. Not to be overlooked are the animals, including rare and endangered species, at the Smithsonian's National Zoo.

You can spend many happy hours and days in the Smithsonian museums. If your time is very limited, on the other hand, you can focus quickly on a few of the most celebrated exhibits. Information desks in the Smithsonian Building (known as the Castle for reasons that are architecturally apparent) and in each individual museum are staffed with volunteers eager to help you find the things you most want to see—whether the Hope Diamond or a dinosaur skeleton; the Wright brothers' Flyer or the First Ladies' gowns; the Star Spangled Banner or a touchable moon rock. The range of exhibits is extraordinary, as this guidebook makes clear.

The sunburst emblem on the cover of this book signifies the power of knowledge—and the Smithsonian's dedication to knowledge. We are also dedicated to pairing learning with delight. I hope, therefore, that you will delight in your visit to the Smithsonian and will carry home with you many treasured memories.

Robert McC. Adams
Secretary, Smithsonian Institution

THE MALL

A long, open, grassy stretch from the Capitol to the Washington Monument, the original Mall was a key feature of Pierre L'Enfant's 1791 plan for the city of Washington. He envisioned it as a "vast esplanade" lined with grand residences. Before the Smithsonian Institution Building (the Castle) was constructed in the mid-19th century, however, the Mall was used mainly for grazing and gardens. To the west, beyond the spot where the Washington Monument now stands, were tidal flats and marshes. (After these were gradually filled in, the Mall was officially extended in this century to the Lincoln Memorial.)

In 1850 New York horticulturist Andrew Jackson Downing was commissioned to landscape the Mall, but his design, calling for curving carriage drives amid a grove of American evergreens, was only partially realized. By 1900 the Mall had deteriorated; its eyesores included a railroad station with sheds, tracks, and coal piles. Two years later, work was begun to implement L'Enfant's early concept, and over the years much of his vision has become reality on a National Mall distinguished by rows of great museum buildings.

On the Mall today people jog, fly kites, toss Frisbees—and just stroll. Near the Castle, in season, children ride on an old-fashioned carousel. For a time each summer, the colorful Folklife Festival takes over. The Mall is also a place where visitors can rest on benches while deciding which of the Smithsonian museums to visit next.

NOTE Because the Smithsonian is a growing, constantly changing institution, some of the exhibits described in this book are themselves subject to change from time to time. In addition, special temporary exhibitions continually come and go. **PLEASE INQUIRE AT THE INFORMATION DESK IN EACH MUSEUM FOR THE LATEST WORD ON CHANGES IN THAT BUILDING.**

A statue of Joseph Henry, the Smithsonian's first Secretary, occupies a place of honor in front of the north entrance to the Smithsonian Building—the colorful red sandstone Castle on the Mall.

THE SMITHSONIAN— WHAT IS IT?

Smithsonian Institution Building
Jefferson Drive at 10th Street, SW
Open every day of the year except December 25, 10 a.m. to 5:30 p.m.
Telephone: (202) 357-2700

There is a widespread misconception that the "Smithsonian" consists mainly of a single red sandstone building that resembles a castle. On the contrary, the Smithsonian is contained in many buildings—and is many things. Centered on the Mall in Washington, D.C., where most of its buildings are located, the Smithsonian also has museums and operates facilities elsewhere in the Nation's Capital, as well as across the country and around the world.

First of all, the Smithsonian Institution is the world's largest complex of museums and art galleries, with holdings in every area of human interest totaling more than 100 million objects and specimens. These range from a magnificent collection of ancient Chinese bronzes to Muhammad Ali's boxing gloves; from the gowns of the First Ladies to the Apollo Lunar Landing

AT A GLANCE

The first place to go for Smithsonian orientation is the **Visitor Information and Associates' Reception Center** in the Great Hall of the original Smithsonian Institution Building, the Castle (see page 13). Few exhibits are to be found in this building, however, much of it being closed to the public and given over to administrative offices and the Woodrow Wilson International Center for Scholars. The tomb of James Smithson is adjacent to the Jefferson Drive entrance to the Castle.

Authentic down-home country music has often been featured at the Smithsonian's Festival of American Folklife, a popular celebration of America's splendidly diverse cultural heritage. Traditional music and craftspeople from all over the nation and abroad attract visitors by the thousands to the Mall each year.

Module and a 3.5-billion-year-old fossil. The scope is staggering, and even seemingly trivial objects serve a serious purpose in furthering understanding, interpreting the past, and establishing a historical record.

Only about 1 percent of the Institution's holdings are on display at any one time, the rest being used behind the scenes by scholars and scientists as they work to increase our knowledge of science, art, and history, for the Smithsonian is also a major center of basic and scholarly research. Expeditions are made to all parts of the world to gather new facts and specimens, and a large publications program spreads widely the information assembled by all these experts.

In addition, the Smithsonian is deeply involved in public education. Its resources are made available for education and research from the elementary to postgraduate levels. Touring groups of school children are a common sight in the museums. Many Smithsonian programs are carried out in cooperation with universities and other institutions, including government agencies, here and abroad. Through the Smithsonian Associates (see page 156), the Institution offers courses and workshops in a variety of subjects, as well as discovery and study tours and other opportunities to learn and to participate in many activities.

The Smithsonian is also active in the performing arts. Such events as concerts, theater and dance programs, and puppet shows are sponsored by the Resident Associate Program and some of the individual museums. The Smithsonian Cham-

The Buck Hill Quartet, a jazz ensemble—presented in a courtyard concert series sponsored by the Resident Associate Program. This is just one example of the Smithsonian's varied activities in the performing arts.

ber Players and the Smithson String Quartet present a series of concerts each season, for example, often performed on rare period instruments housed in the National Museum of American History. The popular Festival of American Folklife, designed to remind visitors of their cultural heritage, is staged annually.

To say that the Smithsonian is devoted to national service in the arts, sciences, and history is to mean, for example, that it will answer inquiries about the historical importance of an object or the provenance of a work of art; lend objects to other museums; offer technical museum training; circulate traveling exhibitions on many subjects to scores of cities across the nation and overseas; provide reports on phenomena such as volcanic eruptions, earthquakes, animal migrations, and tidal waves; track artificial earth satellites; or help the FBI and police departments identify the age and sex of a murder victim from a skull or femur.

Smithsonian facilities devoted exclusively to research include:

Smithsonian Astrophysical Observatory. Here scientists study the physical characteristics and evolution of the universe. Research is carried out in Cambridge, Massachusetts, at the Center for Astrophysics, which was formed to coordinate research by the Smithsonian and the Harvard College Observatory. The largest field facility is at 8,500-foot Mount Hopkins, 35 miles south of Tucson. Among the research instruments there is the unique Multiple Mirror Telescope, developed jointly with the University of Arizona.

The Washington Monument is a backdrop here for an entry in the Smithsonian's kite-flying contest. (© Lillian M. O'Connell.)

Smithsonian Environmental Research Center. Located seven miles south of Annapolis at Edgewater, Maryland, adjoining the Chesapeake Bay, the Center has a variety of habitats and vegetation—14 miles of shoreline, fresh and brackish marshes, abandoned fields, and forest—for its study of human impact on the environment. Research and educational programs advance knowledge of an estuarine environment and contribute to rational use of land and water resources. For information about public programs offered at the Edgewater site, call 261-4190 in the Washington area or (301) 798-4424.

Smithsonian Tropical Research Institute. Headquarters and laboratories of this facility are in Panama, on the Pacific and Atlantic oceans and on an island preserve, where scientists study the behavior, ecology, and evolution of tropical organisms.

Marine Station at Link Port, Fort Pierce, Florida. The National Museum of Natural History directs research in marine science here.

Conservation and Research Center, National Zoo. Located on more than 3,000 acres near Front Royal, Virginia, the center hopes to conserve endangered and exotic animals by means of research on captive breeding and behavior.

Archives of American Art. Letters, sketchbooks, and diaries of American artists are contained in the archives, along with the records of collectors, art historians, curators, and museums. The documents are preserved in Washington, with microfilm centers in New York, Detroit, Boston, San Francisco and Los Angeles. For information, call (202) 357-2781.

Here, samples of water are being taken at Edgewater, Maryland, for a study of the effects of agriculture and human use on the Chesapeake Bay. The relationship between people and the natural environment is the focus of the Smithsonian Environmental Research Center, one of the research facilities.

Origin and Structure

The Smithsonian owes its origin to James Smithson, an English scientist who never visited the United States but who nevertheless willed his entire fortune to this

Designed by Edward Durell Stone, the massive Kennedy Center stands on a 17-acre tract overlooking the Potomac River adjacent to the Watergate complex. Under its roof are five theaters: the Eisenhower Theater (primarily legitimate stage); the Opera House (opera, musical comedy, ballet, modern dance); the Concert Hall (symphony concerts, recitals); the Terrace Theater (experimental drama, poetry readings, chamber music, children's presentations); and the American Film Institute Theater. The red-carpeted Grand Foyer is lit by 18 crystal chandeliers and dominated by a giant sculptured head in bronze of President John F. Kennedy. Three dining facilities serve lunch and dinner. Free guided tours are given daily from 10 a.m. to 1:00 p.m., and there is pay parking underneath the building. Telephone: (202) 254-3600.

country "to found at Washington, under the name of the Smithsonian Institution, an Establishment for the increase and diffusion of knowledge among men."

Smithson died in Italy in 1829, and his bequest of more than half a million dollars—a great fortune in that day—was received with mixed feelings in Washington in 1838, stirring up a lengthy debate in Congress as to whether the nation should, or indeed could, legally accept the funds and accompanying trust. After studying the matter for eight years, Congress decided to accept the bequest, but also determined that the federal government lacked the authority to administer such a trust directly. As a result, it created a corporate entity, "The Establishment," to take charge of the Smithson will. This body, in effect constituting the Smithsonian Institution, consisted of the President of the United States, the Vice President, the Chief Justice, and the heads of the executive departments. To actually govern the Institution, a board of regents was created, along with the position of Secretary of the Smithsonian.

The Smithson bequest was deposited in the United States Treasury and the government agreed to pay 6 percent interest on it to the Smithsonian in perpetuity. In the formal creation of the Smithsonian, provision was made for work in areas that have continued to be of concern—science, art, history, research, museum and library operation, and the dissemination of information.

In taking action on Smithson's bequest, Congress said that its purpose was to provide for "the faithful execution of said trust

An artist's aerial view of the Quadrangle complex, with the Smithsonian Castle in the background and the Arts and Industries Building at far right. The entrance pavilion to the Arthur M. Sackler Gallery is at left and the one to the National Museum of African Art is at right, both facing Independence Avenue. The International Center's entrance kiosk is at the far left center of this watercolor.

agreeable to the will of the liberal and enlightened donor.'' In this way, the United States Government solemnly bound itself to the administration of a trust, and the relation of the government to the Smithsonian became as a guardian to a ward.

Thus the Smithsonian today is a national institution that receives substantial support from the federal government as well as essential funding from private sources, including the Smithson endowment. Control rests in the Board of Regents, which is composed of the Chief Justice of the United States, the Vice President, three members each from the United States Senate and House of Representatives, and nine private citizens. The board elects the Secretary of the Smithsonian, who is the administrative head of the Institution. Included under the aegis of the Smithsonian, but separately administered by their own boards of trustees are the **National Gallery of Art** (see page 119), the **Woodrow Wilson International Center for Scholars,** and the **John F. Kennedy Center for the Performing Arts.** The Wilson Center, located in the Smithsonian Building, was established by Congress in 1968 as a living memorial to President Woodrow Wilson and serves as an international institute for advanced study. The Kennedy Center, on Rock Creek Parkway at New Hampshire Avenue and F Street NW, was created by Congress in 1958 as the National Cultural Center, and was designated in 1964 as a memorial to the late President Kennedy.

The Castle

The red sandstone Smithsonian Institution Building, with its eight crenelated towers, symbolizes the entire Institution to many visitors. Popularly known as the Castle, it was designed in Norman style by James Renwick, Jr., architect of Grace Church and Saint Patrick's Cathedral in New York and the Renwick Gallery in Washington (see page 137).

A disastrous fire in 1865—just 10 years after the Castle was completed—destroyed the upper story of the main building and the north and south towers. Three hundred portraits of Indians and many personal belongings of James Smithson were among the valuable objects lost to the flames. It took two years to restore the building. In the 1880s much of the Castle was remodeled and enlarged, and in recent years, many of its rooms have been restored and furnished with Victorian period furniture.

In the beginning, the Castle housed all the Smithsonian's operations, including a science museum, lecture hall, art gallery, research laboratories, administrative offices, and living quarters for the Secretary and his family. Today the Castle is used largely for the Institution's administrative offices, including the Secretary's, and it is also the home of the Woodrow Wilson International Center for Scholars. Of particular interest to the visiting public is the fact that the very helpful Visitor Information and Associates' Reception Center is located in the Castle.

Near the Jefferson Drive entrance to the building is the tomb of founder James Smithson.

The Quadrangle (opening 1987)
A major new facility for exhibition, research, and education, known as the Quadrangle complex, occupies a 4.2-acre site bounded by the Castle, the Freer Gallery of Art, Independence Avenue, and the Arts and Industries Building.

Two major museums are located here, the Arthur M. Sackler Gallery (see page 93) and the National Museum of African Art (see page 101), as well as the International Center and an education center with classrooms, an auditorium, and workshops for public programs. Offices of the Smithsonian National and Resident Associate programs and the Smithsonian Institution Traveling Exhibition Service (SITES) also are located in the building.

Remarkably, 97 percent of this vast structure is underground. Because of its compelling architectural design, however, visitors never have the sense of being in a dark and dreary "basement." To overcome any such perception, the design incorporates abundant natural light from skylights; dramatic descents, via escalators and staircases; a spacious skylighted concourse connecting the various classrooms and offices of the third level; and indoor fountains and attractive plants.

Above ground are entrance pavilions for the two museums—pyramidal roof for the Sackler Gallery, rounded for the Museum of African Art—and a small, bronze-domed circular structure called the kiosk, through which visitors enter the International Center, classrooms, and other public areas.

These attractive entrance buildings are incorporated into the Enid Haupt Garden, named for its donor, philanthropist Enid Annenberg Haupt. Covering the entire Quadrangle site and resting atop the massive structure below, this magnificent ornamental area features a winter Oriental garden, a summer Islamic garden, a small rose garden, and a 100-year-old European linden tree (which was protected during the construction of the complex). In the center is a large Victorian parterre. More than 100 pieces of 19th-century garden furnishings, many from the time the Castle and the Arts and Industries Building were still young, are included in the design.

The International Center
Occupying the central portion of the third level of the Quadrangle building is the International Center, which sponsors major exhibitions, research, scholarly programs, seminars, films, lectures, and other events focusing on all cultures of the world, especially the non-Western world. Public programs and scholarly symposia augment the exhibitions.

An International Gallery, a symposium hall, and four seminar rooms are used for the public and for scholarly meetings on subjects relating to Smithsonian research interests or to the theme of the current International Gallery exhibition. Many of the International Center's programs are developed in conjunction with the National Associate or Resident Associate programs.

THE SECRETARIES

Nine men of achievement have served as Secretary of the Smithsonian, each having contributed in his own way to the formation and character of the Institution.

Joseph Henry, a famous physical scientist, and a pioneer and inventor in the field of electricity, served as founding Secretary from 1846 until his death in 1878. Under his guidance, the Smithsonian's course was set for the "increase and diffusion of knowledge" with a particular emphasis on science.

Spencer Fullerton Baird, a naturalist, succeeded Joseph Henry as Secretary in 1878, serving until his death in 1887. Baird developed the early Smithsonian museums and promoted the amassing of natural history specimens and collections of all kinds.

Samuel Pierpont Langley, whose particular interests were in aeronautics, astrophysics, and astronomy, launched the Smithsonian in those directions during his years in office, 1887–1906.

Charles Doolittle Walcott, a geologist and paleontologist, was Secretary from 1907 to 1927.

Charles Greeley Abbot, Secretary from 1928 to 1944, was a specialist in solar radiation and solar power.

Alexander Wetmore, an ornithologist, succeeded Dr. Abbott in 1945. Under his administration, the National Air Museum and the Canal Biological Area (now the Smithsonian Tropical Research Institute) joined the Institution.

Leonard Carmichael, a physiological psychologist and former Tufts University president, held office between 1953 and 1964. During those years, the National Museum of History and Technology (now American History) opened and the National Cultural Center (now the John F. Kennedy Center for the Performing Arts) was added as a separate bureau.

S. Dillon Ripley, biologist, ecologist, and authority on birds of the Far East, served from 1964 to 1984. Under his leadership, the Smithsonian expanded greatly in many directions. A number of museums were added, including the Hirshhorn Museum and Sculpture Garden, the Museum of African Art, the Renwick Gallery, and the Cooper-Hewitt Museum. The National Air and Space Museum moved into a magnificent new building. The Ripley administration's crowning achievement is the Quadrangle complex. Secretary Ripley encouraged innovative ways of serving a wide public, including creation of the Smithsonian Associates, the Anacostia Neighborhood Museum, and the American Folklife Festival.

Robert McC. Adams, the incumbent Secretary, is an anthropologist, archeologist, and administrator, who was on the faculty of the University of Chicago from 1955 until coming to the Smithsonian in 1984. His principal research interests concern the agricultural and urban history of the Near and Middle East, the geographical and archeological study of settlement patterns, and the economic and social history of premodern societies. He is best known for his studies in Mesopotamia, site of one of the world's earliest civilizations, where his investigations, along with those of others, have revolutionized the understanding of the rise of urban societies in Mesopotamia. Secretary Adams was provost of the University of Chicago from 1982 to 1984. He also served two terms as dean of the university's Division of Social Sciences, and eight years as director of the university's Oriental Institute. Under his stewardship at the Smithsonian, the Quadrangle complex has been completed and its diverse programs in exhibition, research, and education have been initiated.

Wright brothers' Flyer: In this historic airplane—on December 17, 1903, at Kitty Hawk, N.C.—Orville Wright made the first successful powered and controlled flight by man in a heavier-than-air craft.

Apollo Lunar Module, the backup to the first spacecraft flown in orbit, and similar to Apollo 11's Eagle.

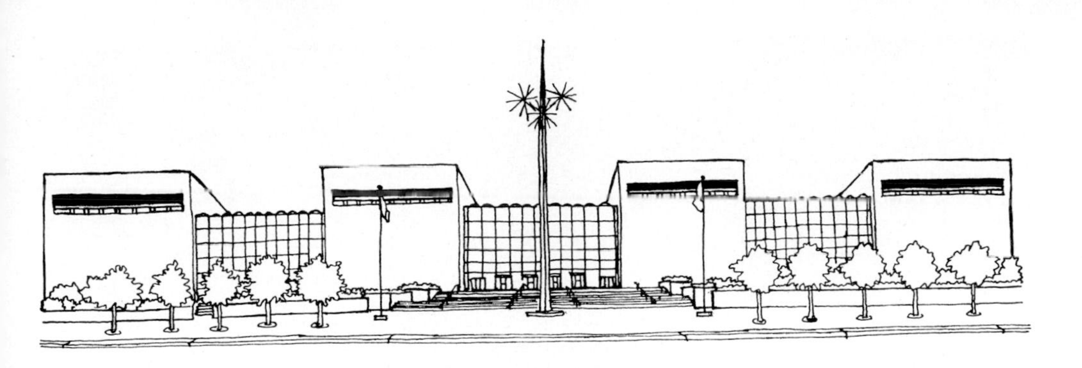

NATIONAL AIR & SPACE MUSEUM

Independence Avenue at 6th Street, SW
Mall entrance: Jefferson Drive at 6th Street, SW
Open every day of the year except December 25, 10 a.m. to 5:30 p.m.
(Extended spring/summer hours determined annually)
Telephone: (202) 357-2700

Information Desk In the Independence Avenue lobby.
Tours Individuals may join public tours daily at 10:15 a.m. and 1 p.m.; no advance reservations needed. Tours for school groups (25–125 persons) and other organizations must be scheduled at least two weeks in advance. Call (202) 357-1400.
Where to Eat Cafeteria on third floor is available until a new cafeteria and a service restaurant open on the first floor.
Museum Shops Near the Mall entrance and on the second floor. Books, postcards, slides, posters, models, souvenirs, T-shirts, and first-day stamp covers are for sale.
Films and Planetarium Shows Special films on flight are projected onto a giant screen; continuous showings daily. Presentations can be seen in the Albert Einstein Planetarium daily. There is a nominal admission fee.

AT A GLANCE

The Wright brothers' **Kitty Hawk Flyer,** Lindbergh's **"Spirit of St. Louis,"** John Glenn's **"Friendship 7," Apollo 11 Command Module, Skylab Orbital Workshop** (visitors can walk through this actual space station to see how astronauts lived in orbit)—these are just a few of the attractions in this vast and exciting museum. Not to be missed are special films on flight projected in spectacular fashion on a screen five stories high and seven stories wide. **"To Fly"** is a world-famous and breathtaking cinematic experience.

The Space Mural—A Cosmic View. This detail from Robert McCall's 75-foot-wide mural, on view in the lobby, shows an Apollo astronaut standing triumphantly on the moon's surface, holding the American flag.

Young or old, flight buff or harried tourist, everyone who has walked through the National Air and Space Museum has shared a unique and memorable experience. Here is an astounding assemblage of aircraft, spacecraft, and related artifacts for visitors to see—but the experience involves more than that. There is a sense of history relived, horizons expanded, optimism rekindled, pride reborn, wonder renewed.

In telling the story of flight—of aeronautics and astronautics—the museum offers 23 galleries, each devoted to a single subject or theme. Visitors are surrounded by visual excitement—theaters, large and small; slide and puppet shows; dioramas and diagrams; and a myriad other innovative devices that invite participation by the public. Overhead and all around are suspended aircraft, rockets, and spacecraft.

The museum's collection encompasses more than 300 historic or technologically significant aircraft, 100 spacecraft, 50 missiles and rockets, 425 aero engines, 350 propellers, hundreds of scale models, aviation uniforms, awards, works of art, instruments, flight equipment, and many items of memorabilia. Although much of the collection is on display, some artifacts are held in storage and for restoration at the Paul E. Garber Facility (see page 38); a significant number are on loan to other museums.

All the aircraft on display are genuine, the museum is proud to point out. They were actually flown. The spacecraft are almost all genuine, too, except for the few it was not possible to bring back to earth. In those cases, the actual back-up vehicle is exhibited, or a replica made from authentic

Delta Solar, by sculptor Alejandro Otero, was a bicentennial gift from the Venezuelan government. The 48-by-27-foot delta-shaped structure is filled with stainless steel rotary sails that turn in the breeze.

flight hardware. Satellites and space probes are actual flight back-up or test vehicles, as close to the originals as possible. Labels specifically note these distinctions.

The logical place to start a tour of the museum is in the Milestones of Flight gallery at the Mall entrance.

Continuum, *a bronze sculpture by Charles O. Perry, stands outside the Independence Avenue entrance to the Air and Space Museum.*

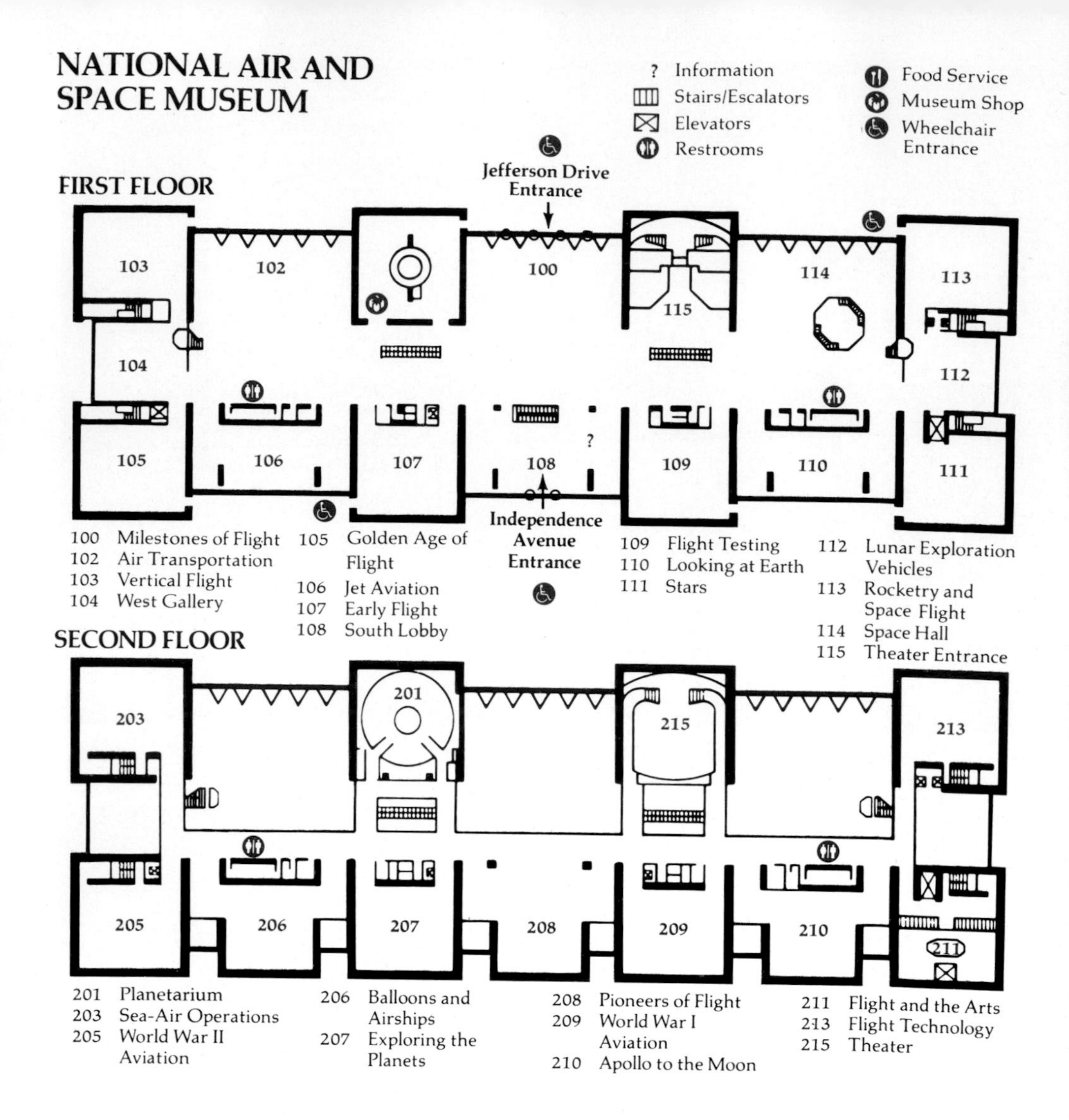
NATIONAL AIR AND SPACE MUSEUM
? Information
Stairs/Escalators
Elevators
Restrooms
Food Service
Museum Shop
Wheelchair Entrance
FIRST FLOOR
Jefferson Drive Entrance
103
102
100
114
113
115
104
112
105
106
107
108
109
110
111
Independence Avenue Entrance
100 Milestones of Flight
102 Air Transportation
103 Vertical Flight
104 West Gallery
105 Golden Age of Flight
106 Jet Aviation
107 Early Flight
108 South Lobby
109 Flight Testing
110 Looking at Earth
111 Stars
112 Lunar Exploration Vehicles
113 Rocketry and Space Flight
114 Space Hall
115 Theater Entrance
SECOND FLOOR
201
203
215
213
205
206
207
208
209
210
211
201 Planetarium
203 Sea-Air Operations
205 World War II Aviation
206 Balloons and Airships
207 Exploring the Planets
208 Pioneers of Flight
209 World War I Aviation
210 Apollo to the Moon
211 Flight and the Arts
213 Flight Technology
215 Theater

A view of the Milestones of Flight gallery, displaying aircraft and spacecraft that have made aviation history.

Gallery 100 **Milestones of Flight**

Theme: Famous airplanes and spacecraft that made aviation history are displayed here on two visual levels.
Highlights—Ground level:
Friendship 7—first U.S. manned orbiting flight, 1962.
Gemini 4—first U.S. space walk, 1965.
Apollo 11 Command Module, *Columbia* first lunar landing, 1969.
Moon rock—collected by Apollo astronauts from the lunar surface.
Viking Lander—proof-test vehicle for the first spacecraft to conduct a detailed study of the surface of another plant (Mars).
Goddard rockets—full-scale model of the world's first liquid-propellant rocket, flown March 16, 1926, and a large rocket constructed in 1941, representing the work of

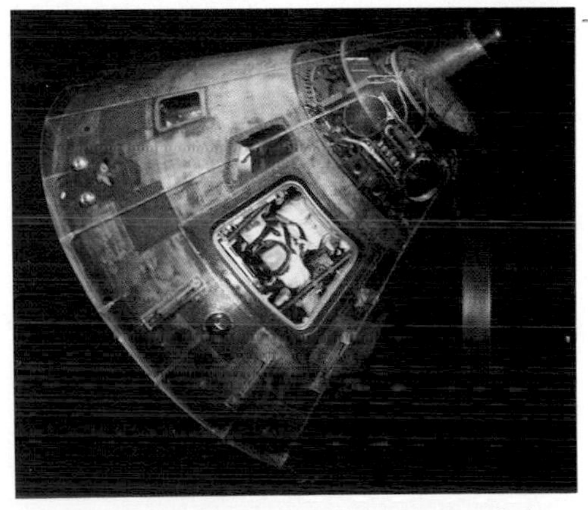

Apollo 11 Command Module Columbia *carried astronauts Neil Armstrong, Edwin E. Aldrin, Jr., and Michael Collins to the moon in July 1969.*

Spirit of St. Louis, *the Ryan NYP (New York to Paris) airplane in which Charles Lindbergh at age 25 made the first solo, nonstop, transatlantic flight, on May 20–21, 1927. The flight took about 33½ hours.*

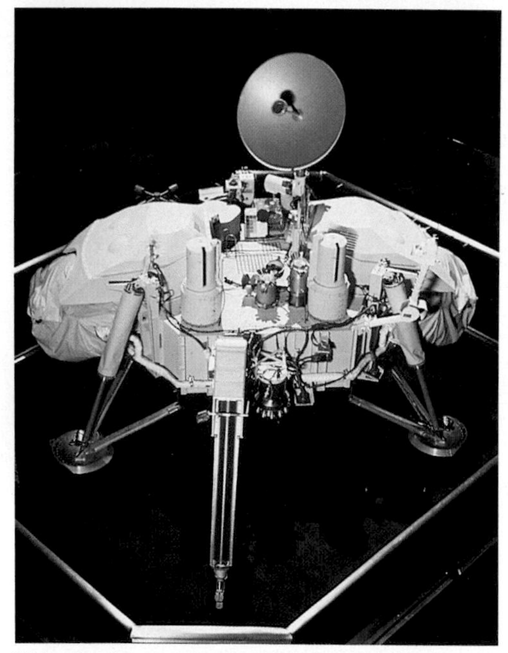

Viking lander, proof-test vehicle for the first U.S. craft to probe the surface of another planet (Mars).

Robert H. Goddard, American rocketry pioneer.

Highlights—Upper level:

Wright 1903 Flyer—Wright brothers' aircraft used for the first powered, controlled, and sustained flight by man in a heavier-than-air craft, 1903.

Bell XS-1 (X-1)—first manned flight faster than the speed of sound, 1947.

Ryan NYP-"Spirit of St. Louis"—Charles Lindbergh's plane, which made the first solo, nonstop, transatlantic flight, 1927.

Explorer 1—back-up model of the first U.S. satellite to orbit the earth, 1958.

Sputnik 1—Soviet replica of the first artificial satellite to orbit the earth, 1957.

Pioneer 10 prototype for the first unmanned spacecraft to fly by Jupiter and out of the solar system.

North American X-15—first winged,

In the Hall of Air Transportation are displayed the DC-3—perhaps the single most important aircraft in air transport history—the Ford Tri-motor, the Douglas M-2, the Pitcairn Mailwing, the Northrop Alpha, the Fairchild FC-2, the Boeing 247 D (the first modern airliner), and other notable aircraft.

manned, aircraft to exceed six times the speed of sound (4,534 miles per hour) and the first to explore the fringes of space, 1967.
Langley Aerodrome No. 5—unmanned research aircraft model, flown successfully, 1896.
Mariner 2—model of the first interplanetary probe to fly by Venus, 1962.
Ad Astra—sculpture by Richard Lippold, at Mall entrance.

Gallery 101 **Museum Shop**

Gallery 102 **Air Transportation**

Theme: Evolution of air transport of people, mail, and cargo.
Highlights
Douglas DC-3—design milestone in aviation—perhaps the single most important aircraft in air transportation history . . . and at 17,500 pounds, the heaviest plane to hang from the museum's ceiling.
Ford Tri-motor—offered dependable, safe, and relatively comfortable service at the time of its debut in 1926.
Douglas M-2—operated on the first air mail route between Los Angeles and Salt Lake City, 1926.
Pitcairn Mailwing—efficient, reliable mail carrier, first used in 1927.
Northrop Alpha—all-metal, cantilever-wing monoplane.
Fairchild FC-2—first nonstop flight from New York to Miami, 1928.
Boeing 247 D—first modern airliner.
Dassault Falcon—executive jet modified for air cargo use.

This is the Northrop Gamma Polar Star, *which made the first transantarctic flight in 1935.*

Douglas DC-7 (nose only)—visitors can walk through the cockpit.

Gallery 103 **Vertical Flight**

Theme: Helicopters, autogiros, special vehicles.
Highlights
Kellett XO-60—Army autogiro for slow flight and near vertical takeoff, 1942.
Focke-Achgelis FA-330—one-man giro-glider, foldable for carrying aboard U-boats, 1942.
Sikorsky XR-4—first helicopter in mass production in the United States, 1943.
Hiller XH-44—first successful U.S. helicopter with coaxial, counterrotating blades, 1944.
Bell LongRanger *Spirit of Texas*—first helicopter to fly around the world.
Rotor-winged aircraft configurations—variations, principles of flight, and control associated with these configurations are explained.
H-34 Marine Helicopter—visitors can look into the cockpit from the surrounding platform.

Gallery 104 **West Gallery**

Theme: Highlighting aircraft of the collection
Highlights
Significant airplanes representing various periods in the development of heavier-than-air flight.

Gallery 105 **Golden Age of Flight**

Theme: Aviation between the two world wars.

Jet engines—from the big Pratt and Whitney JT9D to the tiny Williams WR19—are on display.

Highlights
Beechcraft Staggerwing—Popular general aviation aircraft of the 1930s.
Wittman Buster—air racer that won the most races in aviation history.
Curtiss Robin "Ole Miss"—set endurance record of 27 days over Meridian, Mississippi, in 1935.
Northrop Gamma "Polar Star"—first transantarctic flight, 1935.

Gallery 106 **Jet Aviation**

Theme: The development and present state of jet aviation and its related technology.
Highlights
Mural by Keith Ferris—showing important jet aircraft (size: 20′ × 75′).
Jet engines—a wide range of sizes and performance capabilities, from the huge Pratt and Whitney JT9D used in wide-body jets to the tiny Williams WR19, the world's smallest turbofan power plant.
Films on historic jet aircraft
Lockheed XP-80—first operational U.S. jet fighter.
Messerschmitt Me 262—first jet fighter in combat.
McDonnell FH-1 Phantom I—first operational carrier-based jet.

Gallery 107 **Early Flight**

Theme: The early history of the airplane—from antiquity through the first decade of powered flight.
Highlights
Lilienthal Glider—the glider that inspired Wilbur and Orville Wright.

This whimsical machine, S.S. Pussiewillow II *by British inventor Rowland Emett, is a futuristic space ship, with a control station and hospitality room, a flying carpet, and butterfly-infested paddlewheel.*

Wright Military Flyer—world's first military airplane, 1909.
Curtiss Headless Pusher—a favorite with U.S. exhibition pilots.
Ecker Flying Boat—significant pioneering effort in seaplane design.
Aeronautical engines—the in-line, radial, and rotary power plants that propelled the first airplanes.

Gallery 108 **Independence Avenue Lobby**

Theme: Aeronautical and astronautical trophies, flanked by the two huge murals.
Highlights
Trophies exhibit—includes names of winners and statements about the trophies' histories in the aerospace field.
The Space Mural, A Cosmic View—Robert T. McCall's mural depicting ancient beginnings of the universe, the triumph of lunar exploration, and an optimistic look into the future.
Earthflight Environment—mural by Eric Sloane, dramatically depicting the remarkable ocean of air that is our atmosphere.
Continuum—bronze sculpture by Charles O. Perry, outside lobby entrance.

Gallery 109 **Flight Testing**

Theme: The history of flight research, covering research aircraft and test pilots.
Highlights
Bell XP-59A Airacomet—first U.S. turbojet aircraft.
Hawker Siddeley XV-6A Kestrel—successful application of vectored thrust in an aircraft.
Lockheed Vega "Winnie Mae"—Wiley

Winnie Mae, *noted aviator Wiley Post's modified Vega, was used for stratospheric research in the 1930s.*

Post's Lockheed Model 5-C (modified) Vega, used for stratospheric research in the 1930s.

Gallery 110 **Looking at Earth**

Theme: Combines all the different ways we have studied the earth—from balloons and aircraft to spacecraft.
Highlights
de Haviland DH-4—first of the American World War I fighters, used extensively for reconnaissance and surveying in the 1920s.
Lockheed U-2—the most famous of the reconnaissance aircraft, with flight suit and typical cameras.
Earth Observation Satellites—prototype of TIROS, the world's first weather satellite; ITOS weather satellite; GOES geostationary satellite; models of other satellites and instruments.
Landsat of Your State—interactive touch-screen display showing orbital views of the 50 states.

Gallery 111 **Stars**

Theme: Why travel into space to study astronomy?
Highlights: Space astronomy satellites are able to examine the full range of information coming to us from the sun and stars not adulterated by the earth's atmosphere. Major artifacts include:
Solar Instruments—Orbiting Solar Observatory 1, Solrad, Apollo Telescope Mount;
Stellar Instruments—Uhuru, International Ultraviolet Explorer, Copernicus, IRAS, Space Telescope;
Interactive Experiences—"Fusion Game,"

The Lunar Roving Vehicle allowed astronauts to travel greater distances and carry bulky equipment.

"Birthday Star," "IUE";
Films—"Powers of Ten," "Telescopes of Today and Tomorrow."

Gallery 112 **Lunar Exploration Vehicles**

Theme: NASA lunar-surface exploration.
Highlights—Floor level:
Apollo Lunar Module—a duplicate of the spacecraft that carried astronauts to the surface of the moon in the Apollo program.
Highlights—From the ceiling:
Surveyor Spacecraft—soft-landed on the moon to study lunar soil composition and physical properties of the lunar surface.
Lunar Orbital Spacecraft—circled the moon to perform mapping of the entire lunar surface.
Ranger—provided the first close-up photographs of the lunar surface.

Gallery 113 **Rocketry and Space Flight**

Theme: Science, technology, and man's desire to leave the earth and fly into space—from the 13th century to the present.
Highlights
Historical artifacts and models—representing some of the major contributions in the development of vehicles capable of space flight.
Rocket engines—propulsive devices (solid and liquid propellant) that power space boosters and maneuver spacecraft. Exhibits include forerunners of future exotic rocket systems.
Space suits—from high-altitude aviators' flight suits to fully independent space suits

A view of the Space Hall, showing rockets in the missile pit and a model of the space shuttle orbiter.

Visitors may walk through the Skylab Orbital Workshop, America's first space station.

as used on the moon.
U.S.S. "Enterprise"—Studio model from the "Star Trek" television series.

Gallery 114 **Space Hall**

Theme: Space boosters, guided missiles, and manned spacecraft.
Highlights
Skylab Orbital Workshop—visitors may walk through this back-up Skylab spacecraft, America's first space station. The Skylab group, dominating the hall, includes the Multiple Docking Adapter and Airlock Module.
Apollo-Soyuz Test Project—first international manned space mission.
Viking—America's first sounding rocket developed for scientific purposes.
Aerobee—Major carrier of scientific instruments probing the upper atmosphere.
V-2—first operational long-range ballistic missile.
Jupiter-C and Vanguard boosters—first two U.S. satellite launch vehicles.
NASA Scout—a modern solid-propellant space-launch vehicle.
Minuteman III—U.S. Air Force intercontinental ballistic missile.
M2-F3 "Lifting Body"—used to prepare the way for development of the Space Shuttle Orbiter.
Space Shuttle—16-foot model of the space shuttle *Columbia* on its launch pad, thermal protection tiles, photos, and models of future payloads.

Gallery 115 **Samuel P. Langley Theater**

Special films related to flight are projected

The Blue Angels, the United States Navy's crack aerobatic display team, streak across the Arizona desert in this scene from the breathtaking film To Fly, *an aerial tour of America. (Film courtesy of Conoco Inc.)*

onto a giant screen five stories high and seven stories wide. Spectacular results are achieved with the IMAX projection system. There is an admission fee.

Gallery 201 **Albert Einstein Planetarium**

Simulations of the heavens and of space travel can be seen here. Realistic experiences are produced by use of the Zeiss Model VI planetarium instrument and many auxiliary audiovisual devices. There is an admission fee.

Gallery 203 **Sea-Air Operations**

Theme: Overwater flight, with focus on carrier operations.
Highlights
"Carrier Hangar Deck for All Times"—display of major aircraft from different periods in sea-air history.
Boeing F4B-4—biplane shipboard fighter used from 1932 to 1937.
Douglas SBD Dauntless—principal carrier-based dive bomber used during most of World War II.
Grumman FM-1 Wildcat—first-line Navy fighter at the start of World War II.
Douglas A-4—first-line naval attack aircraft of the 1950s and 1960s.
Aircraft model display—the development of U.S. Navy seaplanes and flying boats is illustrated by handcrafted models.
Ship's Museum—presenting the history of flight over water.

Gallery 205 **World War II Aviation**

Theme: Fighter aircraft from five countries.

Also presented on the big screen at the Samuel P. Langley Theater is The Dream is Alive, *a film featuring the first space walk by an American woman and footage shot by 14 astronauts on three separate space missions. Here, mission specialists Kathy Sullivan and David Leestma (leg stripes) perform activities outside the shuttle. The time. October 5, 1984—Flight 41-G Challenger.*

Highlights
North American P-51D Mustang—an outstanding fighter plane, used in every theater of the war.
Mitsubishi A6M5 Zero—with excellent maneuverability and range, it was used in almost every action throughout the war by the Japanese navy.
Martin B-26, "Flak Bait" (nose only)—flew the most missions of any American bomber in Europe.
Supermarine Spitfire Mark VII—A later version of the legendary British fighter that helped defeat the Germans in the Battle of Britain.
Messerschmitt Bf.109G—principal Luftwaffe fighter; the major opponent of Spitfires and American bombers.
Macchi C.202 Folgore—most successful Italian fighter to see extensive service; used in the African campaign and in Italy and the Soviet Union.

Gallery 206 **Balloons and Airships**

Theme: History of lighter-than-air flight.
Highlights
Objects and prints—testifying to the early preoccupation with achievements of flight through balloons for fun and adventure, followed by military uses for balloons in the American Civil War and the Franco-Prussian War of 1870-71.
Montgolfier Balloon—a working model is demonstrated for visitors.
Double Eagle II—first balloon to make a transatlantic crossing, 1978.
Hindenburg—model of the original (which exploded in flames in 1937).

The Sea-Air Operations gallery features a replica of the hangar deck of an aircraft carrier.

Gallery 207 **Exploring the Planets**

Theme: The history and achievements of planetary explorations, both earth-based and by spacecraft.
Highlights
Voyager—full-scale replica of the spacecraft designed to explore Jupiter, Saturn, and Uranus.
The Viking View of Mars—back-up spacecraft equipment for the Viking landers and computer monitor display of Viking results.
Planetary Weather Report—the weather report for other planets, as would be seen on the nightly news.
Family of the Sun—an animated film for children, taking them on a trip through the solar system.

Gallery 208 **Pioneers of Flight**

Theme: Famous ''firsts'' and record setters.
Highlights
Lockheed Sirius ''Tingmissartoq''—flown by Charles and Anne Lindbergh on airline-route mapping flights, 1930s.
Amelia Earhart's transatlantic Vega—first solo flight across the Atlantic by a woman, 1932.
Wright EX ''Vin Fiz''—Calbraith Perry Rodgers made the first U.S. transcontinental flight in this Wright EX, 1911.
Fokker T-2—first nonstop U.S. transcontinental flight, 1923.
Gossamer Condor—a human-powered aircraft.
Changing exhibits—honoring aviation personalities.

Navigation bridge provides an unusual view of jets being catapulted from a carrier flight deck.

The North American P-51 Mustang was one of the best fighter planes to see action in World War II.

Japan's Mitsubishi A6M5 Zero was noted for maneuverability and speed.

In 1911 Calbraith Perry Rodgers made the first coast-to-coast flight in the Wright EX Vin-Fiz*—from Sheepshead Bay, N.Y., to Long Beach, Calif., in 84 days, and with 70 stops. Speed: about 52 miles an hour.*

Douglas World Cruiser Chicago—first around-the-world flight, 1924.

Gallery 209 **World War I Aviation**

Theme: Technological advances of World War I aviation set against a background of a front-line Allied airstrip somewhere in France, 1918.
Highlights
Aircraft—Fokker D VII, Spad XIII, Spad XVI, and Albatros DVa.
Machine gun synchronization device—a mechanism that allowed the pilot to fire safely through the spinning propeller disc.
Uniforms—those of Gen. William "Billy" Mitchell and Capt. Edward "Eddie" Rickenbacker.

Gallery 210 **Apollo to the Moon**

Theme: Triumph of manned space flight from Project Mercury through the Apollo moon landings.
Highlights
F-1 engine—full size, with cutaway of first-stage engine used on Saturn V rocket.
Astronautical items and equipment—used during the Apollo project.
Information about the moon—selected lunar scenes showing Lunar Rover and astronauts at work.
Saturn booster—models of Saturn 1B and Saturn V rockets.
Lunar samples—four types of lunar soil and rocks.
Space food—a retrospective on how astro-

In 1932 Amelia Earhart made the first solo transatlantic flight by a woman in this Lockheed Vega—from Newfoundland to Northern Ireland in 14 hours, 52 minutes.

nauts' and cosmonauts' food has changed.

Gallery 211 **Flight and the Arts**

Theme: Works of art that record historic events of the aerospace age.
Highlights
Paintings, drawings, prints, sculpture, and photographs from public and private collections. Many works from the NASA collection document U.S. achievements in space.

Gallery 213 **Flight Technology**

Theme: How and why airplanes fly.
Highlights
Design Conference Theater—puppets

A fascinating view of a radial aircraft engine: the Pratt & Whitney R-985 Wasp, Jr., dancing engine.

Five F-1 rocket engines were needed to lift the huge Saturn V vehicle from its launching pad.

The world's first sustained aerial flight was made by two Frenchmen in the Montgolfier balloon in 1783.

illustrate the fundamentals of aircraft design.
Space Technology Theater—project engineer and flight-test engineer reflect on how to overcome the different barriers to flight.
Jet Propulsion Theater—hand puppets relate a fairy tale that develops the topic of jet propulsion . . . a royal family builds a jet-propelled carriage.
Hughes H-1—established the world's speed record in 1935 and the cross-country record in 1937.

Fokker D.VII, a German single-seat fighter plane of World War I, was highly respected by Allied pilots.

PAUL E. GARBER FACILITY

See:
Lockheed P-38J Lightning
Republic P-47D Thunderbolt
Vought F4U-ID Corsair—just a few of the famous fighter planes of World War II on view.
Boeing B-29 *Enola Gay*—the Superfortress from which the first atomic bomb was dropped.
Curtiss JN-4D Jenny—an aircraft made famous by the barnstormers.
North American F-86A and MiG-15—arch rivals in the Korean War.
Able-Baker Missile Nose Cone—the original nose cone of the Jupiter launch vehicle that carried the first monkeys (Able and Baker) into space on May 28, 1959.
Minuteman III ICBM Guidance and Control System—the brain of the Minuteman missile, the standard U.S. land-based intercontinental ballistic missile.

All these and more are on display in the Paul E. Garber Preservation, Restoration, and Storage Facility in Suitland, Maryland, which houses the National Air and Space Museum's reserve collection of historically significant airplanes and spacecraft.

Though the facility has been used since the mid-1950s as a storage and restoration center, only recently have some of the buildings been opened to the public as a "no-frills" museum. Exhibited here are approximately 147 aircraft as well as many spacecraft, engines, propellers, landing gear, and other flight-related objects. Guides conduct tours that include a behind-the-scenes look at the workshop where all phases of the restoration process are handled—from upholstery repair to engine construction.

Formerly known as the Silver Hill Museum, the facility was renamed in 1980 for Paul E. Garber, Historian Emeritus and Ramsey Fellow of the National Air and Space Museum, who joined the Smithsonian Institution in 1920 and was responsible for acquiring a large portion of the aeronautical collection.

Tour Information

Free tours are available Monday–Friday at 10 a.m.; Saturday and Sunday at 10 a.m. and 1 p.m. Reservations must be made at least two weeks in advance. Call (202) 357-1400 between 9 a.m. and 5 p.m., Monday through Friday, or write: Tour Scheduler, National Air and Space Museum, Washington, D.C. 20560.

Individuals or groups of up to 40 will be accepted for the guided tours, which last about two hours. Special tours for handicapped visitors are available upon request. Note: there is no heating or air conditioning in the warehouse-type exhibit areas.

Grumman F8F Bearcat Conquest I.

Hawker Hurricane IIC, a British World War II fighter.

At present, there are five hangar-type buildings open to the public at the Paul E. Garber Preservation, Restoration, and Storage Facility in Suitland, Maryland. A Stearman Trainer of World War II is in foreground.

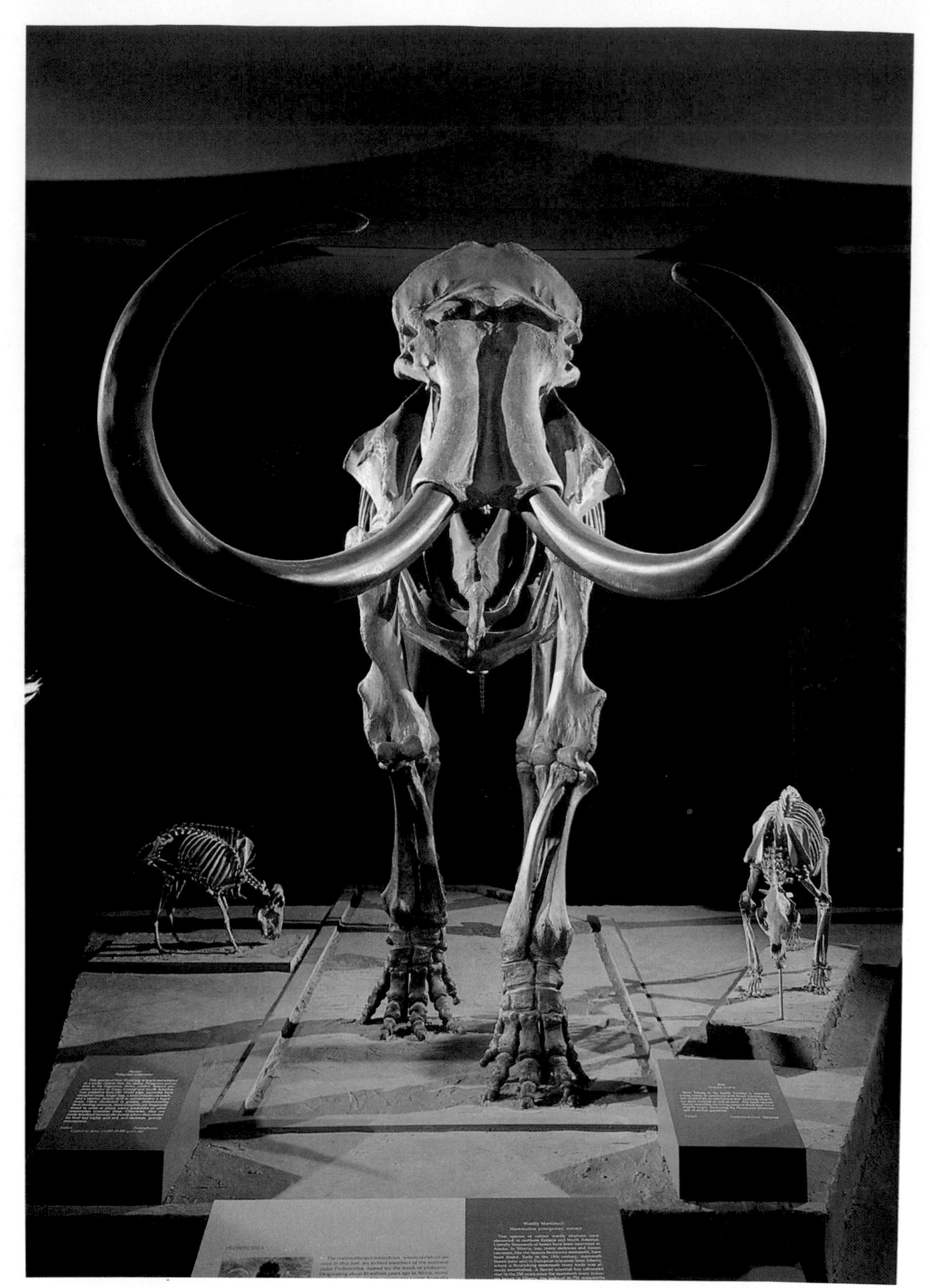

The woolly mammoth—an extinct elephant species that once abounded in North America and northern Eurasia—reached gigantic size during the Ice Age. This skeleton is on display in the Ice Age hall.

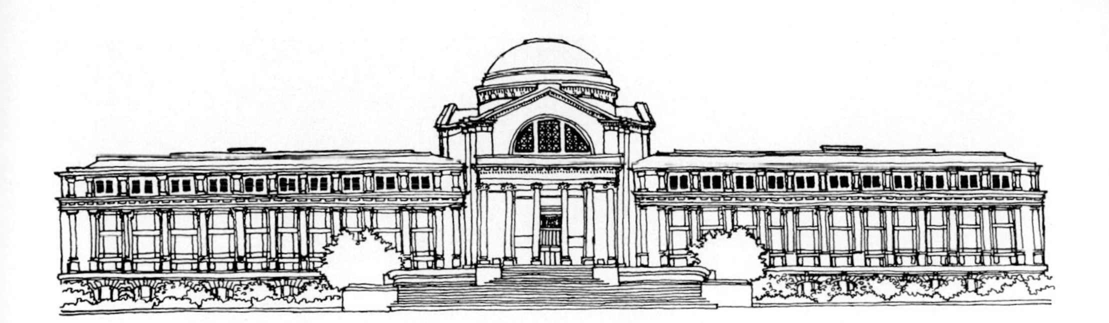

NATIONAL MUSEUM OF NATURAL HISTORY

NATIONAL MUSEUM OF MAN

Constitution Avenue at 10th Street, NW
Mall entrance: Madison Drive between 9th and 12th Streets, NW
Open every day of the year except December 25, 10 a.m. to 5:30 p.m.
(Extended spring/summer hours determined annually)
Telephone: (202) 357-2700

Information Desks Near the Mall and the Constitution Avenue entrances.

Tours Guided public walk-in tours are given at 10:30 a.m. and 1:30 p.m. seven days a week, September through June. There are museum lesson tours for school groups during the academic year; requests must be made in writing well in advance of planned visits. Call (202) 357-2747 for application form.

Audio Tours Receivers for a self-guided audio tour of the exhibits are available in the rotunda on the first floor.

Where to Eat A cafeteria is located off the rotunda on the first floor. The Court, a private dining room open only to Smithsonian Associates, is near the Baird Auditorium on the ground floor.

Museum Shop Located near the cafeteria off the rotunda, this shop offers a wide selection of books on natural history and anthropology for adults and children. Postcards and posters, jewelry, crafts, and other museum-related objects are also for sale. A small gems and minerals shop is on the second floor.

AT A GLANCE

The **Hope diamond,** the **African bush elephant, Diplodocus**—towering over other dinosaurs—**American Indian exhibits, mummies, a coral reef,** and the **Insect Zoo** are among the most popular exhibits in this museum of man and nature. Of special interest here, too, is the **Discovery Room**—where visitors of all ages can see, touch, feel, smell, and taste a variety of natural history specimens—and the unique **Splendors of Nature** exhibit, a celebration of the beauty of the world of nature.

Children love to climb on "Uncle Beazley," the life-size fiberglass model of a Triceratops dinosaur on the Mall outside the Natural History Museum. Inside is an impressive display of dinosaur skeletons.

Discovery Room In this special exhibits area, on the first floor, visitors may touch, feel, smell, and taste objects from the world of nature. Hours: Monday–Thursday, noon to 2:30 p.m.; Friday, Saturday, and Sunday, 10:30 a.m. to 3:30 p.m. On weekends and some holidays, free passes are distributed at the Mall (first floor) information desk. Groups (more than five persons) are not admitted during regular hours; children require chaperones, one adult for every two to three children. For group-reservation application form, call (202) 357-2747.

Naturalist Center Designed for amateur scientists, students, teachers, artists, and collectors, this facility has collections of rocks, animals, plants, and anthropological materials that can be handled in a behind-the-scenes museum atmosphere. Microscopes and other scientific instruments and reference books are available as study aids. Children under 12 cannot be admitted and groups larger than six are not permitted without advance permission of the Center manager. Hours: Monday through Saturday, 10:30 a.m. to 4 p.m.; Sunday, noon to 5 p.m. Inquire at information desk or call (202) 357-2804.

Learning Center and Gallery Classrooms for Smithsonian Associates and school groups, along with a small area for special exhibits, are on the ground floor, off the Constitution Avenue foyer. Inquire at information desk.

The National Museum of Natural History/National Museum of Man is the nation's largest research museum, responsible for maintaining and conserving a treasure house of more than 80 million specimens of plants, animals, rocks and minerals, fossils, and human cultural artifacts. This encyclopedic collection is an essential resource for the nation's scientific enterprises, providing fundamental documentation for the study of the history of life, earth sciences, the biological living world, and human origins and cultures.

The nucleus of the collection was acquired in the 19th-century by U.S. Government expeditions that helped open up the American West and the Pacific. Today, the influx of collections continues through gifts, purchases, expeditions of museum scientists, and deposits from other government agencies.

Only a tiny portion of the museum's holdings are on public display at any one time. The bulk of the collection is stored behind the scenes in laboratories, offices, and storage areas, where it serves as the focal point of research conducted by the museum's staff of 115 scientists and their colleagues from universities, other museums, and U.S. Government agencies.

GROUND FLOOR

To the right, as you enter the museum from Constitution Avenue, are the Learning Center and the Naturalist Center (inquire at the nearby information desk for directions). Straight ahead is a large area for special exhibits and beyond that, the Baird Auditorium, used for lectures, concerts, films, and other special events.

Birds of the District of Columbia Region

An 1829 engraving of an original Audubon watercolor of a swallow-tailed kite marks the entrance to this exhibit, located in the hall outside the Baird Auditorium. Almost 300 mounted species representative of the birds of the eastern United States are shown here, including some superb examples of hawks and eagles. (See page 54 for the description of the main "Birds" exhibit on the first floor.)

FIRST FLOOR

Dominating the rotunda is a giant African bush elephant, a mounted specimen of the largest and most powerful land animal in the modern world. This particular elephant weighed about 8 tons and stood 13 feet, 2 inches at the shoulders.

Colorful banners that mark the locations of exhibit halls here and on the floor above hang all around the rotunda. In the following pages, the exhibits are described in a general right to left sequence, starting from the Mall entrance.

Fossils: The History of Life

This major exhibit area presents a series of highlights illustrating the history of life from its beginnings in the sea 3.5 billion years ago.

Earliest Traces of Life—the first highlight—includes the oldest fossil, a cabbage-sized 3.5 billion-year-old mass built by microorganisms; an animated film on the origin of life; and a new mural depicting life on the primitive earth.

Time and Fossils, a 27-foot-high time column, features an index of geological time and a spectacular mural tracing the evolution of life.

Bengal tiger, believed to be the largest ever taken in India (11 feet, 1 inch long; weighed 857 pounds), is displayed near the Museum Shop off the rotunda.

NATIONAL MUSEUM OF NATURAL HISTORY
NATIONAL MUSEUM OF MAN

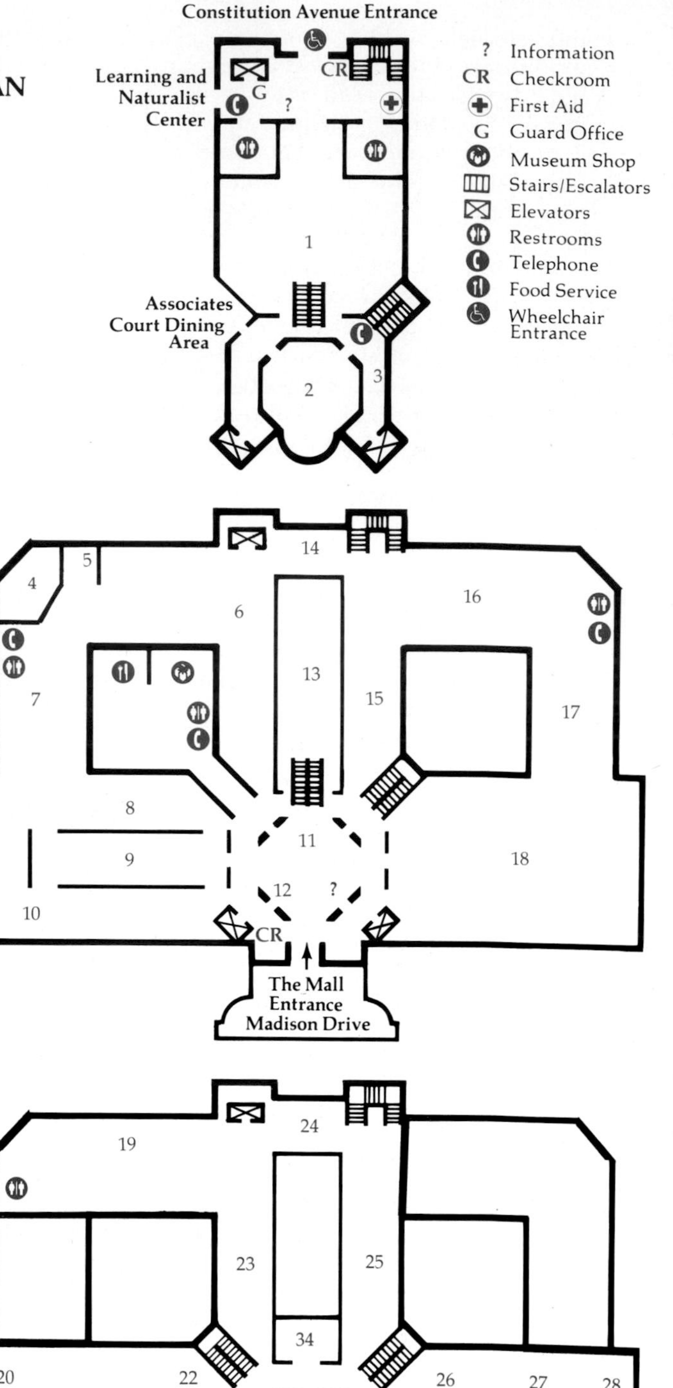

GROUND FLOOR

1 Evans Gallery, Special Exhibits
2 Baird Auditorium
3 Birds of Washington

FIRST FLOOR

4 Discovery Room
5 Discovery Gallery, Special Exhibits
6 Native Peoples of the Americas
7 North American Mammals
8 Birds of the World
9 Life in the Sea
10 The World of Mammals
11 Rotunda (including African Bush Elephant)
12 Recorded Tour Desk
13 Dynamics of Evolution
14 Splendors of Nature
15 Cultures of the Pacific and Asia
16 Cultures of Asia and Africa
17 Ice Age Mammals and the Emergence of Man
18 Fossils: The History of Life (including Dinosaurs)

SECOND FLOOR

19 Western Civilization
20 Reptiles
21 Insect Zoo
22 Bones
23 Human Origin and Variation
24 North Gallery, Special Exhibits
25 South America: A Continent and Its Cultures
26 Earth
27 Moon
28 Meteorites
29 Jade
30 Gems (including Hope Diamond)
31 Minerals
32 Fossils: The History of Life
33 Rotunda Gallery, Special Exhibits
34 Dynamics of Evolution

An African bush elephant—the largest land animal of modern times—greets visitors in the rotunda.

This mural in the "Earliest Traces of Life" exhibit depicts life on the primitive earth approximately 3.5 billion years ago. Scientists envision the planet at that time—when the earliest known life began to appear—as having been volcanically active, with erosion proceeding rapidly on the barren terrain. Dotting the shallow waters are moundlike living structures known as stromatolites, formed by communities of growing algae. Other algal life forms lend a green tint to the waters of hot springs.

This is an overall view of the dinosaur gallery, which is dominated by the 80-foot-long skeleton of Diplodocus, *a member of the sauropod family, the largest land-living animals ever to have walked on the earth.*

Life in the Ancient Seas documents the dramatic explosion of hard-shelled life at the beginning of the Paleozoic Era, 600 million years ago. It includes a display of the rare 530-million-year-old fossilized soft-bodied animals of the Burgess Shale. Among the Smithsonian's greatest scientific finds, these fossils were discovered at a site in British Columbia in 1910 by the Institution's fourth Secretary, geologist Charles D. Walcott.

The Conquest of Land presents fossils of some of the earliest plants and animals to make the transition from life in water to life on land. Among the many fascinating specimens here are a 16-foot-tall fossil of one of the earliest trees, *Callixylon;* trees and smaller plants from the ancient coal forest of North America; and skeletons of many early amphibians. The section closes with displays on the seed and the amnionic egg—the two evolutionary innovations that secured the conquest of land for plants and animals.

The emergence of flowering plants about 120 million years ago led to profound changes in the nature of land life; today, flowering plants make up the vast majority of the earth's vegetation. In the highlight called **Flowering Plants,** there are fossils of many early ancestors of the plants we now depend on so greatly. Life-size models of early flowering plants are represented in a walk-through diorama of a scene on the Potomac River from the early part of the Cretaceous Period, about 105 million years go.

Reptiles—Masters of the Land includes skeletons of dinosaurs, the great reptiles that dominated the earth for 140 million years before their extinction about 65 million years ago. *Diplodocus,* an 80-foot-long member of the sauropod family of dinosaurs, the largest land-living animals ever to have appeared on the earth, towers over skeletons of *Camptosaurus, Stegosaurus,* and the newly mounted *Antrodemus,* a fearsome predator.

Several highlights are displayed on balconies overlooking the Dinosaur hall. **Flight** deals with the evolution of adaptations for flying and presents a magnificent life-size model of a pterosaur with a 40-foot wingspan. **Living Fossils** exhibits living forms of plants and animals—such as alligators, horseshoe crabs, and gingko trees—that are nearly identical to their fossil ancestors.

Shark! displays the reconstructed jaws—5 feet high and 4 feet wide—of *Carcharodon megaladon,* a 40-foot-long great white shark that lived 5 million years ago. The shark's 48 front teeth, some 5 to 6 inches long, were donated by a fossil collector. The jaws and teeth of a modern great white shark are displayed nearby for comparison.

Fossils as Natural Resources presents 12-foot-high natural outcrops of five vitally important fossil resources: coal, oil, limestone, diatomaceous earth, and phosphorite.

Mammals in the Limelight focuses on the spectacular explosion of mammalian evolution following the extinction of dinosaurs about 65 million years ago. A series of four huge murals recreates scenes of animal and plant life in successive epochs of the Age of Mammals. The murals provide settings for numerous fossil specimens, including mounted skeletons, many of them assembled from fossils unearthed in the past century and a half in the American West by Smithsonian scientists. The different stages of horse evolution are shown through fossil specimens, an animated film, and a mural.

Ice Age Mammals and the Emergence of Man

This hall gives a glimpse of mammals and man during the Ice Age, one of the most extraordinary periods in the earth's history. At the entrance, a cast of a 24,800-year-old mammoth tusk, beautifully engraved by an early artist, symbolizes man's emergence at this time as a dominating influence on the environment. A small audio-visual theater shows the process of glaciation and how, over the past two million years, colossal ice sheets repeatedly scoured and transformed the surfaces of the continents.

Reconstructions of the largest Ice Age mammals dominate the hall: a giant

Soaring over the dinosaur gallery is a life-size model of a pterosaur with a 40-foot wingspan. These flying reptiles disappeared from the earth along with the other dinosaurs some 65 million years ago.

ground sloth, a woolly mammoth, and an Irish elk. Also to be seen here is an Ice Age bison (freeze-dried by nature) that was recovered by Alaskan gold miners.

Archeological sites in Africa and Europe are reconstructed to show successive phases of man's biological and cultural evolution during this period. A remarkable, life-size tableau of a Neanderthal burial shows that at least 70,000 years ago man's ancestors buried their dead and may have believed in an afterlife.

African, Asian, and Pacific Cultures
Push a button at the Music of Africa showcase and hear drums, zithers, and other tonal instruments being thumped, shaken, or strummed. At the same time, slide projections show the instruments being

The 20-foot-tall giant ground sloth, weighing several tons, lived in the Americas during the Ice Age.

In this reconstruction of a Neanderthal burial in Regourdou Cave, France, about 70,000 years ago, the body of a young man has been put on a bear skin in a stone-lined pit. Offerings of bear meat and stone tools were then placed on a slab above the body and covered with rocks. Wood was set on top, and a funeral fire was lit.

played amid the background of tribal rhythms.

Another display offers visitors an opportunity to step into a reproduced Herero hut from southwestern Africa to join the Himba people who are also visiting in the home. Softly bowed Himba music can be heard in the background. Not far away is the Initiation Dance diorama, showing Luvale boys being initiated into manhood by masked elders. Many other exhibits cover aspects of hunting and farming; religion, arts, and music; crafts and textiles.

Crafts and objects from daily life of peoples of northern Africa and the Middle East are to be seen in other cases in this area. The religions of Islam and Judaism are spotlighted here.

A charming central display in the area covering various nationalities of Asia shows everyday objects in the forms of Japanese folk crafts. A figure representing Bali, Monkey King of Kish Kindhya, performs a sacred dance drama of India. A stunning diorama presents a scene from a Chinese opera.

There are also Shinto and Confucian shrines and an iron Buddha from Korea. Other exhibits tell something of Oriental music, calligraphy, and language. Objects of daily life from Tibet, China, and the Ryukyus are shown along with a room from a Korean house. Still other exhibit cases deal with the music and crafts of Thailand, India, and Pakistan. One display is devoted to the ancient Cambodian Khmer culture and another presents the delightful shadow puppets of Malaysia.

Luvale boys (Angola, Zaire, and Zambia) are initiated into manhood by masked elders in a ceremonial dance.

One of the famous massive stone heads from Easter Island stands at the entrance to the Pacific Islands area, devoted to the native peoples of Indonesia, Melanesia, Polynesia, Micronesia, Australia, New Zealand, and the Philippines.

Among the exhibits are a diorama showing tattooing as practiced by the Maoris of New Zealand, and two of the stone discs used as money on Yap in the Caroline Islands. Other displays feature boomerangs and bark paintings by aborigines of Arnhem Land, descriptions of sailing and fishing in Polynesia, and rice growing in the Philippines.

Splendors of Nature

Unlike the museum's other exhibits, this one tells no scientific story; its specimens simply are intended to dazzle viewers with their beauty and are here just to be enjoyed. Among the ''splendors'' are fantastic crystal formations, rare and exquisitely colored shells, beautifully detailed fossils, iridescent butterflies, exotic insects, live orchids, and elegantly crafted Indian and Eskimo artifacts made of natural materials.

Dynamics of Evolution

In this hall is an impressive array of preserved specimens, skeletons, skins, and shells—all from the museum's study collections and all examples of the great diversity of life that has come about through evolution. The process of evolution is explained here, providing a framework for understanding other exhibits in the museum.

A prominent tower of human faces

A stone head from Easter Island, South Pacific.

makes it immediately clear that there is a great deal of variation among living organisms. The role of genes and DNA in producing this variation is explained with family photographs of three and four generations, models of snapdragons, and a short film.

A life-size diorama of an eastern woodland scene convincingly demonstrates the struggle for existence as predators stalk their prey, and plants and animals compete for space and food. In the section on natural selection, two male elk in a diorama battle for a watching female, and insects and other animals display the camouflage evolved to protect them from predators or the vivid "warning" colorations that signal harmfulness to predators. Two polar bears highlight the evolution of new species.

In this scene from a traditional Chinese opera, advisers warn the queen mother of a plot to usurp the throne of the infant emperor of the Ming dynasty.

Bali, Monkey King of Kish Kindhya, Hindu mythological figure, performs a sacred dance of India.

Crystals of the mineral elbaite, with quartz and albite, from Tourmaline Queen Mine, California.

Precious wentletrap (Epitonium scalare *Linnaeus), a marine snail shell from the Pescadores.*

These walrus tusks were carved by Eskimos at Nunivak Island, Alaska (collected before 1957). All three of the exceptionally beautiful specimens pictured on this page are on display in the Splendors of Nature hall.

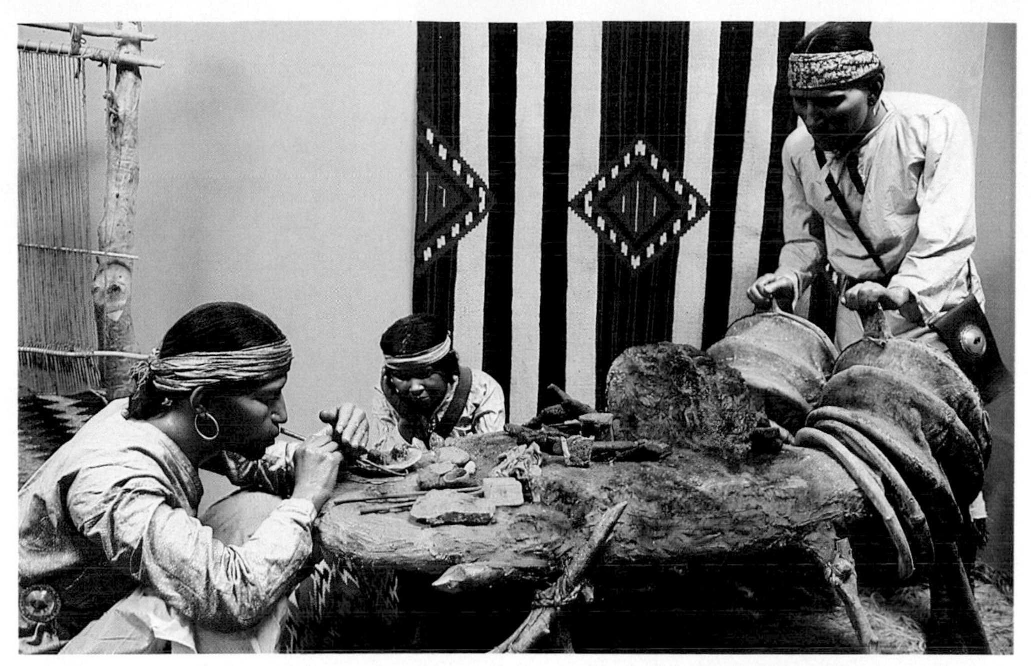

Navaho weavers and silversmiths are shown at work, about 1890, in this Native American cultures diorama.

A young Eskimo boy has just caught an undersized seal through the ice, much to the amusement of his family, in this diorama in the hall of Eskimo and Indian cultures.

Sioux Indian eaglefeather headdress, about 1880, with ermine tails, horse-hair, and beadwork.

Eskimo and Indian Cultures
Off the rotunda, at the entrance to this hall, is a mural depicting individuals of representative tribes from various time periods, organized geographically from Point Barrow in the Arctic to Tierra del Fuego and Cape Horn. The hall is arranged according to cultural areas—regions within which the Native American cultures were broadly similar through shared histories and adaptations to similar environments.

The Arctic, the first region shown, opens with a diorama of a Polar Eskimo family laughing at the young son who has just caught an undersized seal through the ice. This is one of the earliest American Indian life groups prepared for the museum; it was first displayed at the turn of the century.

Next are exhibits of Eastern Woodland cultures, with objects ranging from a birch-bark canoe to tomahawks and lacrosse sticks (Indians invented lacrosse).

In the Plains Indians exhibit there is a teepee made of buffalo hides and decorated with porcupine quills. This teepee was obtained for the 1876 Centennial Exposition in Philadelphia, just at the end of the buffalo-hunting era. At the far end of this hall are some of the best Northwest Coast art objects to be found in any museum.

Around the corner in another part of the hall are exhibits of the historical Indian cultures of California, the southwestern United States, Mexico, Guatemala, the Andean region, Panama, the West Indies, the South American tropical forest, Patagonia, and Tierra del Fuego.

Discovery Room
Here is a room that appeals to the curious of all ages. Elephant tusks, petrified wood, woolly mammoth teeth, coral, and hundreds of other natural history objects are set out on the floor, on tables, or in boxes where they may be touched and closely examined. There are even items to smell and taste (a collection of coriander, sesame, fennel, and celery seeds). Staffed by volunteers, the room is open a limited number of hours each day. Inquire at the information desks for hours and directions.

Birds
Specimens from all over the world are dis-

A view of the Discovery Room—where visitors may see and handle a wide variety of natural history objects.

Penguins of the Antarctic: this scene in the Birds hall is based on photographs taken near Little America.

played here in realistic settings, with their differences in form, size, and color emphasized. Exhibits illustrate migration, reproduction, feeding habits, flight, and ways in which birds have been important to man.

Birds of special interest are shown in their habitats: the appealing Antarctic penguins; the ostrich, complete with babies just out of their eggs; and the argus pheasant, noted for its enormous plumes. Birds are shown that were once abundant in North America but became extinct by the hand of man, including the penguinlike great auk, the Carolina parakeet, and the passenger pigeon. Though numerous as recently as the 19th century when they darkened the sky while flying overhead, not a single passenger pigeon remains alive today, the last having died in captivity in 1914.

Sea Life

At the rotunda entrance to this hall are two 3,000-gallon aquarium systems housing living microcosms of two fascinating ocean environments—the subarctic waters of the Maine coast and the tropical coral reefs of the Caribbean.

Based on more than 20 years of field and laboratory research by a Smithsonian scientist, these two systems use a variety of electronic, mechanical, and biological devices to simulate natural conditions on the reef and on Maine's rocky coastline. The colorful inhabitants of the reef tank include living corals, tangs, parrot fish, crabs, and the blue-green, green, and red algae "turf." By contrast, the cold-water tank contains kelp, rockweed, marsh grass, lobsters, scallops, mussels, hake, tomcod, and scaup. Both tanks are working laboratories used by scientists seeking a better understanding of how wild ocean communities function.

"Blue Planet," a 15-minute film showing Smithsonian research in coastal Maine waters and in the Caribbean, is shown continuously in a small theater near the two microcosm systems.

Hanging in this hall is the largest single exhibit in the museum, the life-size, 92-foot-long model of a blue whale—the biggest animal that has ever lived and now an endangered species. Behind it, other whales are shown in outline, illustrating their sizes and shapes, and all around it are models of sharks, sailfish, and porpoises.

Fish, crustaceans, corals, mollusks, sponges, and other preserved specimens of sea life are on view, including a rare exhibit of a giant squid—a sea animal that for centuries has stimulated imaginations and given rise to fantastic tales and myths. Only the third giant squid ever recovered on the United States coast, it is preserved in the same condition as when found after being washed ashore on Plum Island, Massachusetts, north of Boston, in February 1980.

Smithsonian scientists are diving in submersibles to study biological frontiers beneath the ocean. Hydrolab, the stationary underwater laboratory that revolutionized oceanographic research by permitting scientists to live and work in the depths of the sea for as long as a week, is on display, by courtesy of the National Oceanic and Atmospheric Administration. A large section of the front of Hydrolab has been opened for the exhibition, exposing scientific instrumentation and furnishings. Three life-size "aquanaut" manikins are in the habitat, giving the illusion that a scientific mission is in progress. Photographs and video footage of scientists at work in Hydrolab are on view.

A few feet from Hydrolab hangs a large model of the three-man deep-diving submersible *Alvin*—three-quarters the size of the actual ship—on loan to the museum from the U.S. Navy. Beneath the model are displayed specimens and photographs of giant tube worms and other unusual deep-sea organisms discovered—by scientists diving in *Alvin*—living and thriving a mile and a half beneath the Pacific Ocean in and around geothermal springs. These organisms constitute the first known communities of higher animals not directly or indirectly dependent on sunlight and photosynthesis for energy. How these organisms derive their energy instead from sulfur compounds—a process called chemosynthesis—is explained by the exhibit, which includes spectacular National Geographic video footage.

At the end of the hall is an imposing mounted specimen of the largest of the fin-footed aquatic mammals—the sea walrus. Here, visitors may watch a delightful film about pinnipeds—a family of mammals that includes the seal and the sea lion, in addition to the walrus.

Mammals

Exhibited in these halls in lifelike settings are hundreds of mammals—one of the largest and most varied groups of animals. (Mammals are warm-blooded, have backbones, hair at some time in life, and nourish their young with milk.) The range is from duckbill platypuses to kangaroos, gorillas, lions with cubs, horses, zebras, antelopes, giraffes, and many, many more. Exhibits explain classifications of the mammals, their environments, and aspects of their relationship to man. At the end of the hall is a montage, "Mammals in Art," showing how humans have portrayed mammals from ancient times to the present.

American Mammals

Twelve large exhibits in one section of this hall show, in true-to-life backgrounds, groups of caribou, wolves, bison, moose, deer, and bears—all native to the North American continent.

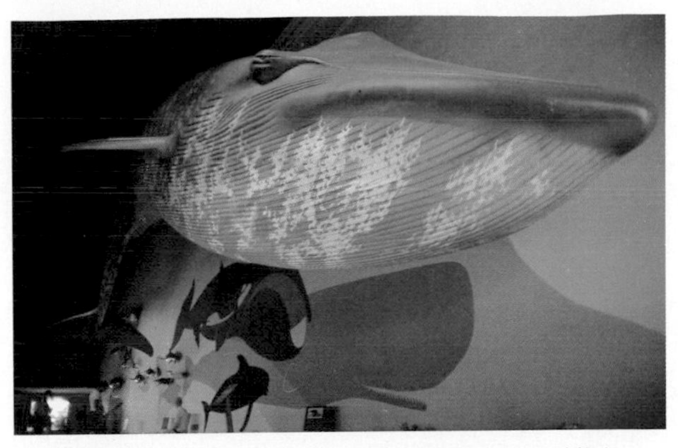

Blue whale—92-foot-long model of the largest mammal living today and probably the largest ever—in the Sea Life hall.

Mountain goats forage on sparse vegetation in the Rockies in this lifelike scene in the Mammals hall.

This is the Hope diamond—the best known and largest (45.5 carats) blue diamond in the world.

Warner Crystal Ball, cut from crystalline quartz, is 12-7/8 inches in diameter; weighs 106-3/4 pounds.

SECOND FLOOR

Minerals and Gems

Gold crystals of extraordinary size and beauty; huge gypsum crystals from the Cave of Swords at Naica, Mexico; a large group of amethyst crystals from Brazil; and a mighty jade boulder, sliced and polished, from New Zealand are among the most spectacular items in the minerals area. Introductory exhibits tell about minerals—how they are formed and their characteristics. Hundreds of outstanding specimens are displayed, including smithsonite, a zinc carbonate identified by James Smithson (see page 10) himself.

Directly ahead, beyond the minerals, is the fabulous **Hall of Gems,** where more than 1,000 exotic and rare cut and polished gemstones are to be seen. The legendary Hope diamond—the visual goal of everyone entering the museum—glitters in splendor in a glass-fronted vault. This 45.5-carat blue diamond was named for Henry Philip Hope of England, who once owned it. Mrs. Evalyn Walsh McLean of Washington was the last private owner, and the diamond is still in the setting made for her. Acquired from her estate in 1949 by the New York jewelry firm of Harry Winston, Inc., the notorious but magnificent gem was given to the Smithsonian in 1959.

While the Hope may be the best known, there are other gems of unique sizes and colors to be seen here: the 127-carat Portuguese diamond; the brilliant blue 423-carat Logan sapphire; the spectacular Rosser Reeves ruby with its unmatched six-rayed star; the 68-carat, champagne-colored Victoria Transvaal diamond; the heart-shaped Eugenie blue diamond; and the 330-carat

"A Geologist's View of the Earth" globe.

Moon rock collected by Apollo astronauts.

Star of Asia, one of the finest star sapphires in the World.

Of particular interest because of their fascinating histories are such jewelry pieces as the Napoleon necklace, the Marie Antoinette earrings (one of the last gifts from King Louis XVI to the queen), and the Empress Marie Louise tiara with 950 diamonds.

A small but elegant hall adjacent to the gems contains a number of the Smithsonian's choice jade carvings, including screens, vessels, bowls, incense burners, scepters, and candlesticks, produced mostly during the Ching dynasty (1644–1912) in China, when the art of jade carving remained at its peak.

Earth, Moon, and Meteorites
At the rotunda entrance to this hall is a large and unusual relief globe described as a "Geologist's View of the Earth." Mountains and plains are identified with colors indicating their ages. Giant underwater ridges, where the crust is splitting apart, and the deep ocean trenches, where the crust is being consumed, are visible features formed by the drifting continents.

Elsewhere in this hall, the great antiquity of the earth is shown by specimens of the world's oldest known rocks, formed nearly 3.8 billion years before early man. Rocks and economically important ores such as copper, gold, and silver—many available to touch—are exhibited with explanations of how they were formed. Our planet's restless nature is shown by a volcano film and a seismograph that records large earthquakes as they occur.

Five moon rocks, returned to earth by the Apollo astronauts, are strikingly displayed in a small area linking the earth and meteorite exhibits. Younger than meteorites but older than the earth's surface, the moon rocks provide a unique record of the first billion years of planetary history.

There are explanations of how lunar rocks reveal ancient cosmic events that affected the entire solar system, such as the tremendous bombardment by huge meteorites that sculpted all of the planets 4 billion years ago. The processes that have destroyed the record of these ancient cataclysms on our planet are shown in the earth hall.

The Smithsonian has the largest collection of meteorites on exhibit in the world. Included in this display are large fragments of extraterrestrial matter that formed Meteor Crater, Arizona, 4,000 feet in diameter and 600 feet deep. These and other meteorites are our best clues to the origin of the solar system nearly 5 billion years ago.

South America: Continent and Culture
This hall shows the distinctive environments and resources of four South American regions and the different ways in which cultures have adapted to them during the Prehistoric, Colonial, and Modern eras. Entering the hall from the rotunda,

Tehuelche Indians, nomadic hunters of the South American grasslands, throw bolas, which entangle prey.

visitors see a mural and diorama of the great Patagonian grasslands as they looked in the 19th century. A hunt is in progress: nomadic Tehuelche Indians, armed with bolas, are riding across the plains in hot pursuit of fleeing rhea birds.

The next environment is that of the tropics. On both sides of the spectator are the giant trunks, branches, and vines of a lifelike tropical rain forest. Despite this lush vegetation, the region supports only marginal agriculture, and the tribes that live in the forest depend heavily on wild foods. The weapons, brightly colored ornaments, and everyday tools of one of the tribes, the Waiwai, are displayed.

Fishing helped support large prehistoric cities along the arid Pacific coastlands. A diorama features a balsa raft of the kind used for thousands of years by these coastal people.

The culture of the high Andean mountain valleys (sustained by abundant potato and corn crops) is vividly portrayed in a three-dimensional re-creation of a town plaza featuring a marketplace and church facade. Objects from the Inca civilization are exhibited beneath a mural of a mountain citadel.

Human Origin and Variation

A definition of physical anthropology marks the entrance to this hall. Exhibits explain how man is distinguished from other primates by characteristics such as upright posture, digital dexterity, and verbal ability. The influence of environment, nutrition, and health on growth and devel-

Artifacts from the hall of Western Civilization: Origins and Traditions include an encaustic portrait from Egypt, used as a mummy mask; a Greek vessel found in Italy; an Etruscan bronze spirit boat, 1000–5000 B.C.; a vessel from an early European farming community; a Roman glass bottle; a Cycladic figurine, 3000–2000 B.C.; an Egyptian cat mummy; Ibis, symbol of the Egyptian god Toth; the head of a king in relief, Ptolomaic era; an Egyptian black-topped pot, 4000 B.C.; flint "daggers" from northern Europe; and a Luristan bronze sword.

opment is illustrated.

There is a special section on mummification here, displaying Peruvian, Egyptian, and Aleutian mummies, plus the remains of Wilhelm von Ellenbogen, an 18th-century Philadelphian, whose tissues turned into a form of soap—a phenomenon that sometimes occurs when groundwater comes in contact with buried bodies.

Stunning, life-size murals dramatize the way people have altered the human body over the ages, including tattoos, pierced lower lips, bound feet, tooth modifications, and ancient Peruvian surgery.

Here, too, is a model of the skull of a two-million-year-old manlike creature—*Zinjanthropus*—excavated by L.S.B. Leakey at Olduvai Gorge, Tanzania, Africa.

Western Civilization: Origins and Traditions

This exhibit traces the increasing complexity of Western civilization from the end of the Ice Age, about 10,000 years ago, to about A.D. 500. Ice Age flint tools, such as knives and projectile points, and a reconstructed cave featuring paintings of animals, illustrate man's early dependence on hunting.

It was after the Ice Age that people in southwestern Asia began the shift to farming as a way of life. A scene from one of the earliest farming villages—Ali Kosh—is re-created in a diorama. Technological advances accompanied the spread of agriculture. Egyptian pottery from 4,000 B.C. is shown, along with increasingly sophisticated stone and bone tools from Europe.

Another diorama re-creates a scene from the Mesopotamian city of Larsa in 1801 B.C.

The growing complexity of urban life fostered a new form of political and social organization called the "state," which eventually led to the formation of empires.

The complexity of ancient societies as reflected in burial customs is illustrated by an exhibition on the tomb of Bab-Edh-Dhra. An accompanying film describes the tomb's excavation by Smithsonian archeologists.

The growth of empires is illustrated with an outstanding collection of artifacts, including pottery and stone tools from Troy, Luristan bronzes, Egyptian mummies and mummy cases, a Cycladic figurine, Etruscan bronzes, Greek pottery, Roman glass, a Roman mosaic, and Roman money.

By about A.D. 500, the basic patterns of Western civilization were set, and many of them persist today. The last part of the hall focuses on this persistence, with a reconstructed modern bazaar scene, a comparison of a Roman cookbook with a modern one, and a fascinating film on the town of Winchester, England, from its Celtic origins through Roman occupation to the present.

Bones

Hundreds of skeletons of animals, birds, reptiles, amphibians, and fishes, ranging in size from the gigantic extinct Steller sea cow to the tiny pocket mouse, are posed characteristically and grouped by orders to illustrate their relationships. Exhibits show how bone structures evolved in adaptation to environment. Horses, for example, developed leg and foot bones that enabled them to run swiftly on the level grasslands where they lived and grazed. The skeleton of a famous race horse, Lexington (1850–1875), illustrates this adaptation.

Reptiles

The subtropical Florida Everglades, home of alligators, tree frogs, turtles, and a variety of snakes, including the diamondback, is one of the life-size habitat displays in this hall. There are specimens of such large snakes as the king cobra, reticulated python, and boa constrictor from the Malayan and Amazonian jungle. Feeding habits, methods of locomotion, and the economic influence on man of reptiles and amphibians are also illustrated.

Insect Zoo

The whirrs, chirps, hisses, and rattles that visitors hear at the entrance to this hall are the sounds of the most abundant, diverse, and successful animals on earth—insects and their relatives. Many of them can be seen in this unique museum-zoo—flying, climbing, or swimming about in their Plexiglas-walled cages. Visitors can watch a leaf-cutter ant colony at work in its fungus garden, look into a real beehive, or touch a giant grasshopper. They can also watch tarantula feedings three times each day. Life history processes, such as metamorphosis, are demonstrated and explained. Keepers who feed and handle the insects answer visitors' questions.

Coffins of Tenet-Khonsu, high priestess of the god Amon-Ra, Egypt, about 1000 B.C.

Among the residents of the popular Insect Zoo is the cone-headed grasshopper of Central America.

Two Insect Zoo visitors, intent on a specimen.

Star-Spangled Banner. This is the flag that flew over Fort McHenry during the attack of a British fleet in 1814 and inspired Francis Scott Key to write the poem that became the words to our National Anthem.

NATIONAL MUSEUM OF AMERICAN HISTORY

Constitution Avenue between 12th and 14th Streets, NW
Mall entrance: Madison Drive between 12th and 14th Streets, NW
Open every day of the year except December 25, 10 a.m. to 5:30 p.m.
(Extended spring/summer hours determined annually)
Telephone: (202) 357-2700

Information Desks Near the Mall and the Constitution Avenue entrances.
Tours and Demonstrations Tours include: "Highlights," "First Ladies Hall," and "Threads of History" (needlework and textiles). Schedules vary seasonally. Demonstrations include Electricity, Pain Clinic, and Spirit of 1776 (daily life during the American Revolution). In the Hands on History Room, visitors may handle reproductions of 18th-century artifacts. Check at information desks for times and changes. For special school and adult tours, call (202) 357-1438; TDD: 357-1563.
Where to Eat A cafeteria and a snack bar are located on the lower level. The Palm Court on the first floor serves ice cream and light refreshments.
Museum Shop/Bookstore Located on the lower level. For sale are a wide variety of objects and publications relating to American history and civilization, along with postcards, film, slides, T-shirts, and posters. Another, smaller museum shop

The **Star-Spangled Banner**, the **Foucault Pendulum**, the **First Ladies' gowns, George Washington's uniform and tent, Whitney's cotton gin, Edison's light bulb, Ford's Model T**—the list could go on and on, for this is a museum as diverse as it is exciting and instructive. On the first floor the emphasis is on the history of science and technology; on the second, social and political history; and, on the third, stamps, coins, glass, ceramics, musical instruments, photography, communication, and graphic arts.

NATIONAL MUSEUM OF AMERICAN HISTORY

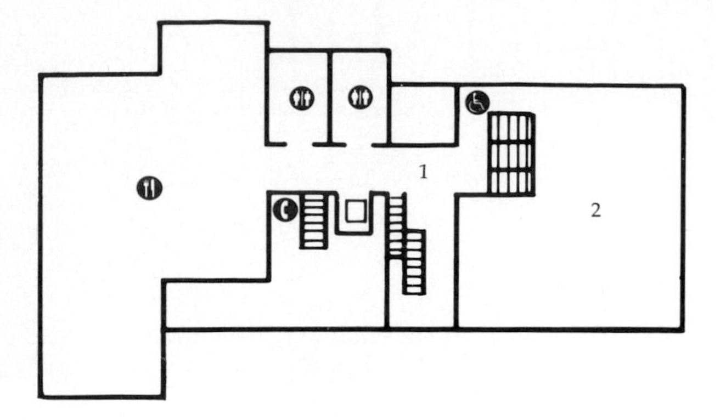

- ? Information
- CR Checkroom
- First Aid
- G Guard Office
- D Discovery Corners and Demonstrations
- Elevators
- Restrooms
- Telephone
- Food Service
- Museum Shop
- Wheelchair Entrance
- Post Office
- Stairs/Escalators

LOWER LEVEL

1 Special Exhibition Gallery
2 Museum Shop/Bookstore

FIRST FLOOR

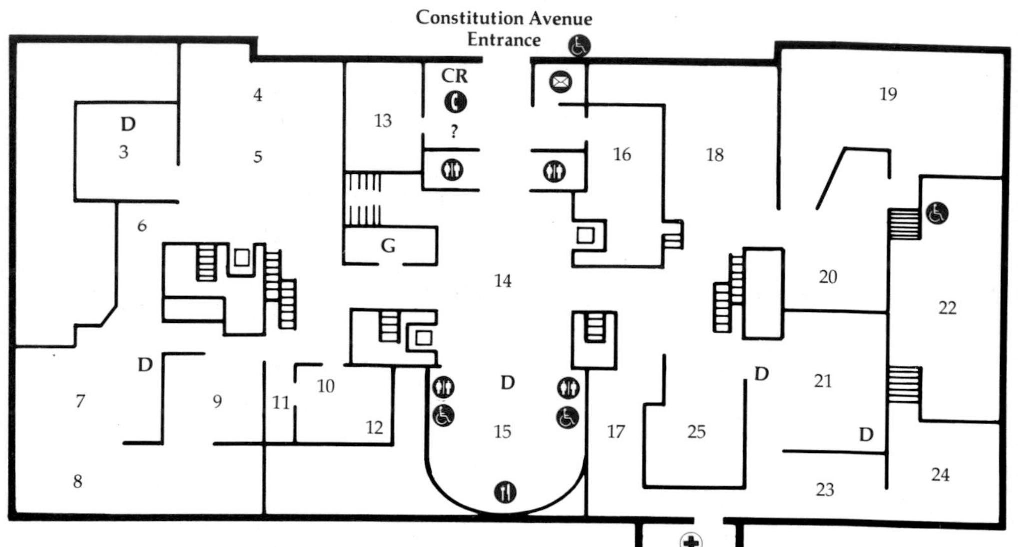

3 Textiles
4 Atomic Clocks
5 Atom Smashers
6 Quilts
7 Pain and Its Relief
8 Medical Sciences
9 Computing
10 Physical Sciences
11 Special Exhibition Gallery
12 Physical Sciences
13 Special Exhibition Gallery
14 Foucault Pendulum
15 The Palm Court
16 Auditorium
17 Timekeeping
18 Agriculture
19 American Maritime Enterprise
20 Road Transportation
21 Electricity
22 Railroads
23 Power Machinery
24 Bridges & Tunnels
25 Engines of Change

SECOND FLOOR

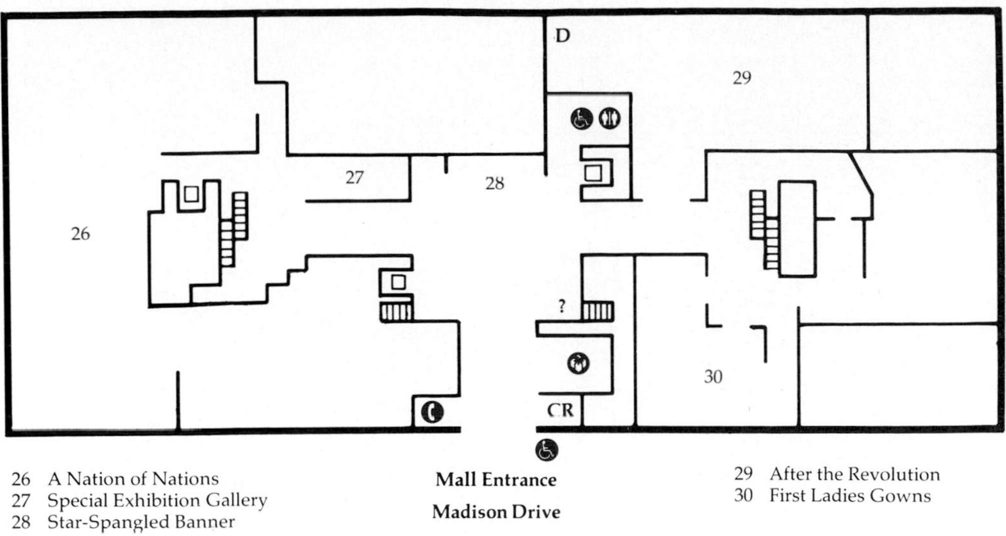

26 A Nation of Nations
27 Special Exhibition Gallery
28 Star-Spangled Banner

Mall Entrance

Madison Drive

29 After the Revolution
30 First Ladies Gowns

THIRD FLOOR

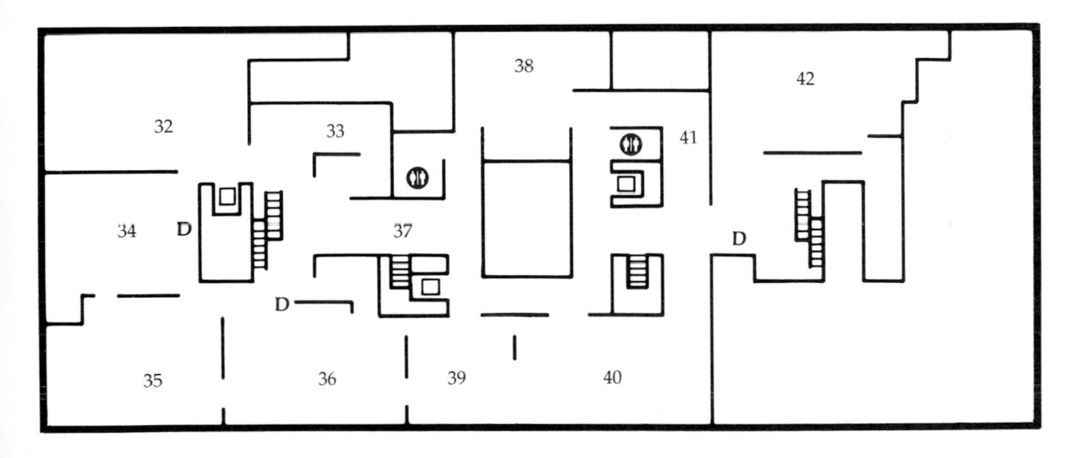

32 Ceramics
33 Glass
34 Musical Instruments
35 Philately & Postal History
36 Printing & Graphic Arts
37 Special Exhibition Gallery

38 Money & Medals
39 News Reporting
40 Photography
41 Special Exhibition Gallery
42 Armed Forces

Country Store-Post Office, near Constitution Avenue entrance. Mail is stamped ''Smithsonian Station.''

is at the Mall entrance.

Smithsonian Post Office Located near the Constitution Avenue entrance in a 19th-century country store. Cards and letters mailed here receive a unique, hand-stamped ''Smithsonian Station'' postmark.

In 1858 the ''objects of art and of foreign and curious research'' in the National Cabinet of Curiosities were transferred from the Patent Office to the Smithsonian—and this was the genesis of the collections in the National Museum of American History (formerly Museum of History and Technology). After the Centennial Exposition of 1876 closed, the Smithsonian's holdings were greatly increased by a windfall of articles that had been displayed in Philadelphia. Many of these objects were put on exhibit in the United States National Museum Building (now the Arts and Industries Building) when it opened in 1881. Today, in this newer museum (which opened in 1964), spacious halls are filled with exhibits that explore America's scientific, cultural, political, and technological history. **Please note that sweeping changes are in progress—and will continue over the next several years—in this building and in the exhibits described here.**

FIRST FLOOR

Country Store Post Office

To the left of the entrance from Constitution Avenue is a country store that was located in Headsville, West Virginia, from 1868 to 1971, serving as a post office for about half those years. Brought to the museum lock, stock, and even barrel (staples and sundries of a bygone era still line the shelves), it again functions as an official post office. Stamps, including special issues, may be purchased here, and mail that is deposited receives a "Smithsonian Station" postmark.

Foucault Pendulum
A crowd is always gathered in the center of the building to watch the Foucault Pendulum, patterned on an experimental device invented by a French physicist in the mid-19th century. Suspended from the ceiling of the fourth floor, more than 70 feet above, a 240-pound hollow brass bob swings back and forth knocking down, one by one, the red markers arranged in a circle around an inlaid compass rose. Although the pendulum's vertical plane seems to change, in fact it remains fixed. What is actually changing its orientation is the floor, which "rotates" under the pendulum because of the earth's rotation.

The Foucault pendulum provides a visual demonstration of the axial rotation of the earth.

Farm Machines
In this exhibition, a wooden plow of colonial times can be compared with later steel plows; the traditional cradle scythe and winnowing fan with a 20-mule-team Holt combine of 1887. The International Harvester cotton harvester ("Old Red") of 1942 symbolizes the transformation of the old labor-intensive cotton culture to one dominated by machines. The internal-combustion tractors illustrate major developments from the 1903 Hart-Parr, to the 1918 Waterloo Boy, to the 1924 John Deere and a more recent International Harvester tractor.

"Old Red," the International Harvester spindle cotton picker (1942), symbolizes the end of the old labor-intensive cotton culture.

Road Vehicles
Among the museum's collection of more than 40 antique automobiles, the rarities displayed here include the Duryea (1893) and the Haynes (1894); a 1903 Oldsmobile; a 1913 Model-T Ford; the 1902 Winton Bullet racing car; and a 1917 White motorbus.

Also on exhibit are vehicles from earlier times, including a handsome 1770 horse-drawn chaise and 19th-century carriages.

The Palm Court is designed to create a turn-of-the century environment for rest, reflection, light refreshments, and popular and light classical music of the period. Reconstructions of Stohlman's Confectionary, a shop of that era, and a Horn and Hardart Automat are incorporated into this attractive area.

Cycles are here too, the earliest a Draisine of 1818. In addition, there are velocipedes, high-wheelers, and safety bicycles. Among the motorcycles on view are the experimental 1869 Roper Steam velocipede and a selection of vehicles manufactured during the first half of the 20th century.

American Maritime Enterprise

This exhibition deals with the history of water-borne commerce, both on the high seas and on America's lakes, rivers, and canals. There are more than 100 ship models, from the *Mayflower* to the most recent Great Lakes ore carrier. The power plant from the 1804 *Little Juliana* is the oldest surviving marine steam engine made in America; the propeller from the 1848 *Indiana* is part of the oldest known screw-propulsion system from a commercial vessel. Machinery salvaged from the U.S. Coast Guard tender *Oak* has been reassembled, enabling visitors to see a fully operational engine room, dating from the early 1930s. There are separate displays relating to disasters at sea, shipbuilding during the world wars, whaling, the China trade, luxury liners, and the seaman's life.

Railroads

The big *1401*—a Pacific-type steam locomotive built for the Southern Railway in 1926—dominates this hall. The Pacific-type was once the most popular general class of passenger locomotive in the country. In contrast to the 280-ton *1401* is the *Pioneer,* a 12½-ton engine of 1851, which served for nearly 40 years on the Cumberland Valley Railroad in Pennsylvania.

This exhibit in the American Maritime Enterprise hall re-creates a typical tattoo parlor for seamen.

Model T Ford of 1913—one of some 15 million of these popular cars built between 1908 and 1927.

NASCAR stock car No. 43 (a 1984 Pontiac) in which Richard Petty won his 200th Grand National race, July 4, 1984, Daytona Beach, Florida.

The 280-ton Pacific-type steam locomotive 1401 *was used on the Southern Railway between 1926 and 1951.*

Harlan and Hollingsworth 42-hp mill engine, used from 1852 to 1927 in a Southern Railway machine shop.

The eight-wheel passenger car of 1836 is the oldest of its type in existence. Scale models are used to trace the development of locomotives and cars, while there are full-scale examples of braking apparatus, couplers, and signaling devices.

At one end of the hall is a Seattle cable car of 1888. Nearby is an 1898 electric street car from Washington, D.C., a diorama of New York's Third Avenue Elevated as it appeared in 1880, and models of other rail-borne vehicles used in urban transit.

Bridges and Tunnels

Displays show the changing techniques of bridge and tunnel construction from the Roman era to the present. There are models of famous bridges of various types —arch, truss, cantilever, suspension—and models also illustrate the variations in tunneling technology. Three major timbering systems common in mid-19th-century tunnels are reconstructed at large scale.

Power Machinery

The full-size engines and models displayed here pertain to the harnessing of atmospheric force (1660–1700); the early age of steam power (1700–1800); and the development of high-pressure and high-speed engines (1800–1920). Exhibits show how steam boilers and the steam turbine evolved, and progress in the techniques of harnessing water power. There are also a number of historic internal-combustion engines.

Hall of Electricity

The first of this exhibition's four parts, *Early Views,* highlights electrostatics and the work of Benjamin Franklin. In a lighthearted tableau showing an 18th-century parlor trick, a lady receives an ''electric kiss'' from a gentleman whose hand touches a large electrostatic machine. *Person to Person* considers the contributions of Samuel Morse, Alexander Graham Bell, and others. *Lighting a Revolution* traces the development of electrical power in the late 19th century with special emphasis on the work of Thomas Edison. And, in the *Demonstration Center,* there are periodic demonstrations of electrical apparatus.

Timekeeping, Phonographs, Typewriters, and Locks

A wide variety of historic timekeepers—from sundials to atomic clocks—are displayed here, along with exhibits tracing the development of American clockmaking.

Several early examples of sound-recording and reproducing machines are here too, including one of Thomas Edison's first phonographs (1877), Emile Berliner's 1888 gramophone, and the Victor Talking Machine.

Some of America's earliest typewriters are exhibited in chronological sequence, starting with a 19th-century reproduction of Burt's patent model of 1829.

Many of the locks, keys, bolts, and other hardware shown are remarkable for the artistry that has been lavished on them.

Engines of Change:
The American Industrial Revolution, 1790–1860

With more than 250 original artifacts, this major exhibition brings to life the American Industrial Revolution. It tells the stories of craftspeople, factory workers, inventors, and entrepreneurs, who all made contributions crucial to our modern way of life.

The exhibition begins with a re-creation of the ''Crystal Palace,'' the site of the 1851 World's Fair in London, where the superiority of American technology first won international recognition.

Major sections of ''Engines of Change'' offer case studies depicting the evolving industrial society and the work culture that made this superiority possible. They also present some of the innovations on which the Industrial Revolution was based—new machinery, interchangeable parts, and the factory system.

The Slater spinning frame, the world's oldest operable locomotive, and the Colt revolver are among the objects that illustrate the ingenuity of the age and the effects of industrialization on American life.

"Electric Kiss" tableau, Hall of Electricity. An 18th-century parlor game, with an electrostatic machine.

Physical Sciences

These exhibits include instruments used by American scientists in their study of the physical world. Of particular interest are the telescope installed for Maria Mitchell at Vassar College and the workshop of a telescope maker, Henry Fitz of New York. Side by side are chemical laboratories of 1790 and 1890, the earlier one equipped with apparatus used by Joseph Priestley. Nearby is an exhibit that addresses the career of Albert A. Michelson, America's first Nobel Prize winner in physics.

A display of teaching apparatus used in American colleges during the early days of the Republic shows how scientific principles were demonstrated to students. Related exhibits pertain to the tools of surveying, geodesy, oceanography, and meteorology.

Computing and Mathematics

Here are astrolabes, sundials, sectors, and other mathematical instruments used by astronomers, architects, surveyors, and military engineers. Jesse Ramsden's dividing engine of the 1770s is an example of an early device for precision graduation.

Nearby are various digital computing devices, ranging from the ancient abacus to mechanical calculating machines and punchcard systems, as well as mechanical and electronic instruments. An adjoining display of colorful paintings depicts demonstrations of mathematical theorems.

Another display deals with electronic computers of the late 1940s and 1950s, including six pioneering digital computing systems.

Medical Sciences
There are two reconstructed dental offices and a dental laboratory of the 19th and early 20th centuries in the **Section of Dentistry.**

Displays in the **Section of Pharmacy** include a European apothecary shop of the 18th and 19th centuries and a turn-of-the-century American pharmacy. Nearby exhibits pertain to the tools of the apothecary and the history of therapeutics.

The **Hall of Medicine** features microscopes and other medical apparatus, a bacteriology laboratory of the early 20th century, a pioneer mechanical heart, early X-ray machines, a CAT scanner, and other recently developed devices for body imaging.

Textiles
A variety of 19th-century American implements for carding wool, braking flax, scutching, hetcheling, and spinning are on display. The process of weaving an 18th-century-type coverlet is demonstrated on a four-shaft treadle loom.

Rarities include the hand-operated knitting frame of the 1700s and a French Jacquard-equipped loom of the 1840s. Textiles shown include Jacquard-woven pictures and coverlets and a wide range of hand-embroideries of the 18th and 19th centuries, as well as examples of other unusual 19th-century fabrics.

Atom Smashers
High-energy accelerators—''atom smashers''—first enabled the systematic probing and disruption of the central cores of atoms, and now, enormously increased in energy, the probing and disruption of particles composing atomic nuclei. They are the indispensable means for advancing the frontier of knowledge toward the infinitely small, and thus toward the fundamental and universal. The conception, construction, and operation of these machines and of the particle detectors used in conjunction with them is the subject of this exhibit. Entire atom smashers, including the first betatron and the first synchrotron, are on display, as well as components of their mammoth relatives.

A reconstruction of the astronomical clock created by Giovanni de' Dondi of Padua, about 1350.

Electric streetcar of 1898, used on the Seventh Street line in Washington, D.C., until retired in 1912.

A view of the "Atom Smashers" exhibition, which deals with the conception, construction, and operation of these machines as well as particle detectors. The first betatron and the first synchrotron are on display here.

Elias Howe's sewing machine patent model of 1846.

A display of beautifully decorated Christmas trees, such as this one, is a holiday attraction.

Atomic Clocks

Nearby is an exhibit of atomic clocks—timekeeping systems attuned to the vibrations of atoms or molecules. Accurate to within millionths, sometimes even billionths, of a second, atomic clocks are essential for advanced systems used in space exploration, navigation, telecommunications, and many areas of scientific research.

Approximately 80 pieces of equipment and 100 photographs and drawings are on view. Together, they trace the development of atomic timekeeping, from scientific theory to commercial practice.

An authentically restored, fully equipped American drugstore of the turn of the century—on display in the Pharmacy Section, Medical Sciences.

SECOND FLOOR

Star-Spangled Banner

Visitors entering the museum from the Mall confront one of the nation's patriotic symbols, the Star-Spangled Banner. This is the historic flag that flew over Fort McHenry following the successful defense against British naval forces on September 13, 1814. A lawyer named Francis Scott Key happened to be aboard a sloop in the Chesapeake Bay. On seeing that the "flag was still there" by the "dawn's early light," Key was inspired to write a poem that became the words to the national anthem. The flag is displayed with a curtainlike protective cover, which is lowered hourly to a musical and narrative accompaniment.

After the Revolution: Everyday Life in America, 1780–1800

This major exhibition is the first in a series that will transform much of this museum. The guiding concept is based on recent research and reevaluation that stress consideration of the entire society, rather than studies of famous, primarily political, figures and issues.

"After the Revolution" comprises six major sections that illuminate the lives of well-documented families and communities in the 1780s and 1790s. It begins with a multi-media program outlining the diversity of the period and the three major cultural groups that adapted to new ways of life—Native Americans, Europeans, and Africans, both slave and free.

Moving from rural to urban settings, the six sections concentrate on the Delaware farm family of Thomas and Elizabeth Springer and their two daughters; African Americans in the Chesapeake area; the Virginia planter family of Henry and Ann Saunders and their daughter, Betsy; the Seneca Nation of the Iroquois Confederacy; the Massachusetts merchant family of Samuel and Lucy Colton; and the major urban center of Philadelphia.

The exhibition features the Springer log house; parlors appropriate for both the Saunders and Colton families, along with their furnishings. Artifacts, including tools, housewares, textiles, ceremonial and religious objects, document the Afro-American blending of European and African traditions; the struggle of the Seneca and other Iroquois peoples to maintain tradition in the face of radical change; and the diversity of trades, crafts, professions, and ways of life in Philadelphia, the country's major urban center of the 1780s and 1790s.

Also part of this installation are two study galleries for temporary exhibitions; a "Hands on History" room in which visitors can handle reproductions of objects related to the people described in "After

This doll house, a creation of the late Faith Bradford, a records expert at the Library of Congress, represents a romantic view of the life of a large and affluent American family in the early 1900s. Its occupants include Mr. and Mrs. Doll, their 10 children, grandmother and grandfather Doll, a cook, butler, chambermaid, and nurse, along with several dogs and a cat.

the Revolution''; and a performance area for concerts, such 18th-century amusements as puppet shows, and other special programs.

First Ladies' Gowns
Beginning with the hand-painted silk of Martha Washington, dresses worn by First Ladies–wives, daughters, or other official hostesses—of each presidential administration are on display. The hair styles and the sizes of the mannequins closely resemble the individual First Ladies. Though the faces themselves are identical, based on a classical bust of Cordelia by Pierce F. Connelly, the women look decidedly different in their fashionable gowns. The period room settings have been decorated, whenever possible, with authentic White House or presidential furniture and accessories.

Also on display is a large collection of White House china, including tableware used for family and state occasions from Washington to the present.

A Nation of Nations
''. . . here is not merely a nation but a teeming Nation of nations . . .''

Walt Whitman

Thousands of original artifacts and documents are displayed in this exhibition, which suggests the diversity of the people who have come to America over the centuries. ''Nation of Nations'' adds up to a powerful affirmation that America is linked to other countries by an intricate web of cultural ties.

At the outset, early patterns of immigration are explored—from Spain, France, Holland, and England, then from almost

This a room in the 1½-story log house of about 1793 that was lived in by Thomas and Elizabeth Springer and their two daughters, a Revolutionary era farm family of New Castle County, Delaware. Three of the house's walls are from the original Springer home; the fourth, the original of which was destroyed by fire, was carefully reproduced for installation in "After the Revolution: Everyday Life in America, 1780–1800."

every part of Europe, as well as forced immigration by black Africans.

"Old Ways in a New Nation" concerns the increasing flow of immigrants throughout the 19th century—their methods of travel, traditional ways of working, the modes of social organization.

"Shared Experiences in a New Nation" focuses on some of the particularly "American" activities and environments shared by immigrants. They took part together in free public schooling (a room from Cleveland's Dunham Elementary School has been reconstructed here); the process of becoming United States citizens; and the routine of military basic training.

Sports have been important in the American experience, too. Anyone can be a fan, and immigrants' children have had the opportunity to become stars through athletic achievement.

Popular attractions on exhibit in this area have included the Bunkers' chairs from the TV series "All in the Family"; Fonzi's jacket from "Happy Days"; Muhammad Ali's boxing gloves; Judy Garland's slippers; and Charlie McCarthy, the famous puppet.

THIRD FLOOR

Armed Forces History

Uniforms, weapons, flags, and ship models illustrate the origin and growth of the armed forces and the life of the citizen soldier. Highlights include George Washington's field headquarters tent and a Revolutionary War vessel—the Continental gunboat *Philadelphia*—dating from 1776 and the oldest U.S. fighting vessel in existence. Ship models include John Paul

A parlor appropriate for Samuel and Lucy Colton, a wealthy merchant family who lived in Longmeadow, Massachusetts, is also on view in "After the Revolution." The elaborate paneling and fine furnishings reflect such a family's participation in international trade and its comparatively high place in the establishment of that era. Set for an inventory after Samuel's death, the room contains a profusion of objects, including English creamware, a Boston secretary desk, and other New England furniture.

Early American silversmiths of the Revolutionary era made a wide assortment of goods ranging from tableware to costume accessories. Shown here are some types of Philadelphia artisans' silversmithing tools and examples of finished products.

Charlie McCarthy, ventriloquist Edgar Bergen's original wooden puppet, is a popular attraction among the collection of Americana on display in "Nation of Nations." American diversity is a theme of this exhibition.

Pictured here in the First Ladies Hall are (left to right) Nancy Reagan, Rosalynn Carter, Betty Ford, Patricia Nixon, Lady Bird Johnson, and Jacqueline Kennedy. The setting represents the Red Room after its renovation during the Kennedy administration. The curtains, the carpet, and many of the furnishings were actually once used in that room in the White House.

Jones's flagship, the frigate *Constellation* of 1797, Civil War ironclads, and the recently recommissioned USS *Missouri,* the battleship aboard which Japan signed the formal surrender ending World War II.

While the armed forces hall undergoes reinstallation, there will be a small display of the evolution of the infantryman's weapons from colonial days to the present. The theme of the citizen in uniform will be further developed in the completed hall.

Photography
Here are settings depicting milestones of photography: an early darkroom; a scene representing one of the first photojournalists, Roger Fenton, documenting the Crimean War; an early studio; an explorer-photographer at work. On display is a large array of early photographs and still- and motion-picture equipment, along with exhibits showing the works of recognized photographers and the results of different photographic processes and techniques. Also, visitors can operate devices from early penny arcades.

Money and Medals
The story that unfolds here pertains to the evolution of monetary exchange. A special feature is a breathtaking **Gold Room.** In addition to coinages and currencies of many nations, the hall includes a coin-collector's browsing area, and an imaginative children's corner. Among other topical exhibits is one showing forgeries of coins and paper currencies.

News Reporting
This exhibition traces the history of Ameri-

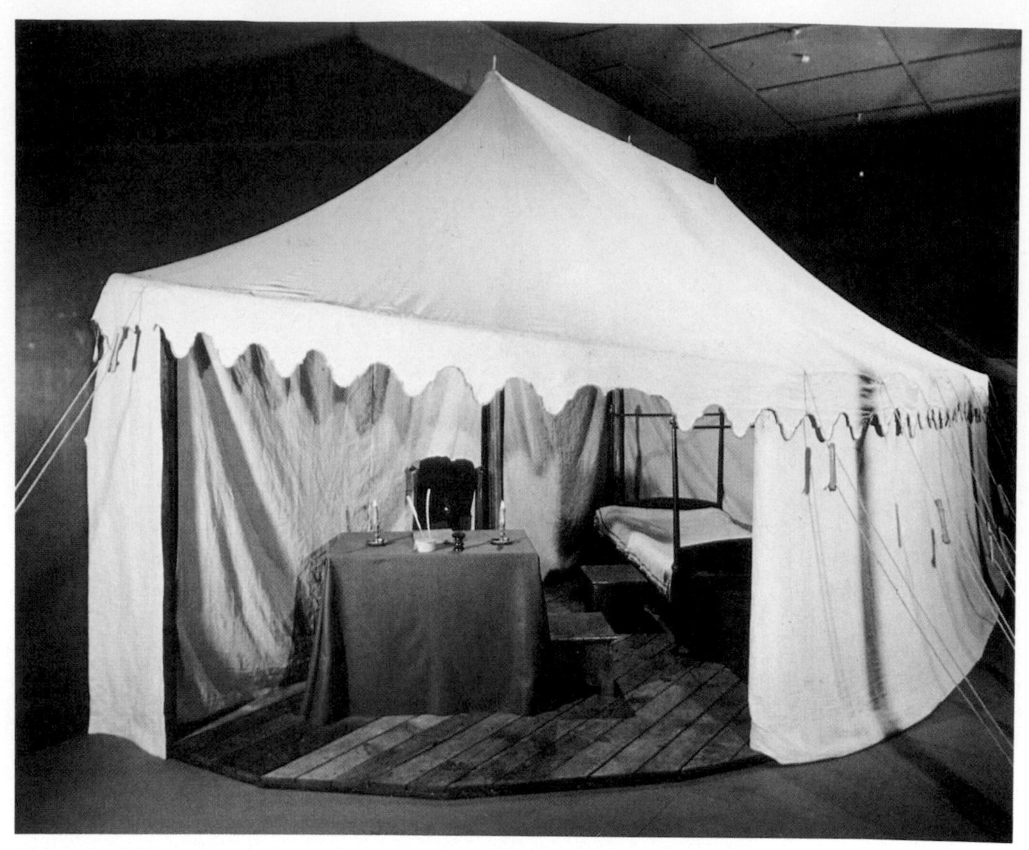

This is the field headquarters tent that was used by Gen. George Washington during the Revolution.

can news reporting and communications technology from the 17th century to the present. Newsreels, television sets, radios, and teletype machines are in operation. Also on exhibit are a space satellite, a special Apollo II moon camera, and rare newspapers, still photographs, and prints.

Printing and Graphic Arts
This hall deals with the history of prints and printing techniques. Demonstrations are staged in four settings. The first is a printing office of Ben Franklin's time, with two wooden presses. Nearby is a 19th-century foundry in which type was still cast by hand, as it had been since Gutenberg's day. A job shop of 1865 is equipped with hand and treadle presses. Inside a newspaper office of the 1880s is a steam-driven Hoe cylinder press.

There also are exhibits on printmaking from the first etchings and woodcuts to modern photomechanical methods. A small gallery features changing exhibits of graphic art and printing techniques.

Postal History and Philately
For the philatelist there is real excitement in the magnificent **National Philatelic Collection,** for more than 75,000 stamps are on display in pull-out frames.

The overall emphasis of the hall is on the development of a postal system to keep pace with the demands of a fast-growing population; topics include the Pony Express and Rural Free Delivery. Finally, there are a number of machines for handling the mail and for producing postage stamps as well as vehicles used in moving the mail.

A special alcove is devoted to philatelic rarities, and a learning center for children

"Franklin Press" from John Watts's print shop in London, where Ben Franklin worked in 1726.

Early gold coin depicting Alexander the Great.

One of the displays in the hall of News Reporting, which is devoted to the history of American journalism.

Snake jug from Anna Pottery, Anna, Illinois, 1876.

A celebrated rarity among U.S. postal issues is this airmail stamp with an inverted center, 1918.

is in a period post office.

Musical Instruments

Displayed in a setting that includes an intimate hall frequently used for concerts and recordings are exquisite examples of Western European and American instruments dating back to the 17th century. Some have been carefully restored to playing condition. In addition to a permanent display of organs, harpsichords, and pianos, there are changing exhibits of stringed, wind, and percussion instruments used in various musical traditions.

Ceramics

Selected for display from among the museum's excellent collection of ceramics are examples from the Hans Syz Collection of 18th-century European porcelain, the Larsen and McCauley collections of English earthenware decorated with American views, American traditional pottery, tableware, and art pottery, and the Leon Collection of yellow-glazed English earthenware. Fine examples from Meissen, Sèvres, Wedgwood, and other important manufacturers can be seen, along with works from Bennington, Baltimore, and Cincinnati.

Glass

On display here is glassware made by ancient Egyptian and Roman artisans; 17th- to 19th-century work from Spain, Germany, Austria, Bohemia, America, Italy, and England; colorful paperweights from Europe and America; French and English cameo glass; and 20th-century Scandinavian wares.

In the American glass exhibits are 18th-century Amelung rarities and examples of Stiegel-type and Gallatin glass; lacy pressed, blown three-mold, and other 19th-century glass manufactured in New England, the mid-Atlantic states, Pittsburgh, and Ohio. The late 19th and 20th centuries are represented by the art glass of Tiffany and Steuben, as well as by fine cut and engraved glass by Hawkes, Libbey, and other manufacturers. Finally, there is a splendid selection of American contemporary studio glass.

Lacy pressed glass dish, New England, about 1830–1845.

Fine musical instruments are heard—in concerts and demonstrations —as well as seen.

Japanese figure, Guardian King of the South (Zōchō-ten), *1185–1333. Wood with polychrome and gilt.*

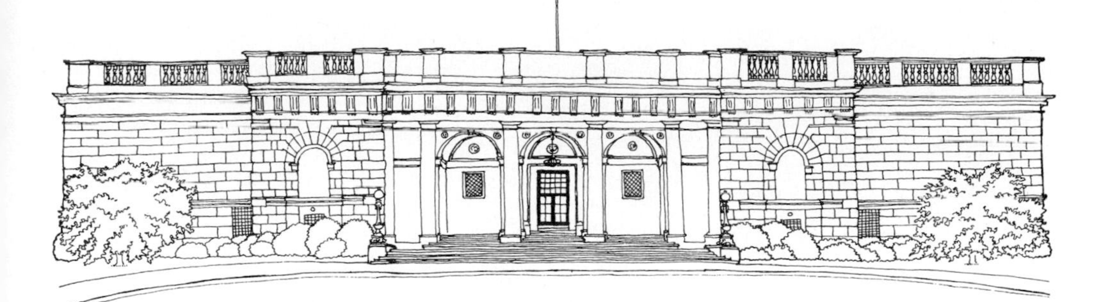

FREER GALLERY OF ART

Jefferson Drive at 12th Street, SW
Open every day of the year except December 25, 10 a.m. to 5:30 p.m.
Telephone: (202) 357-2700

Information Desk Inside the main entrance.
Tours Free guided tours are given daily at specific times. Special group tours must be scheduled at least two weeks in advance. Call (202) 357-3200.
Museum Shop Books, posters, jewelry, cards, and gifts are for sale daily from 10 a.m. to 4:30 p.m.
Lectures Six or seven free public lectures on Asian art are offered annually.
Library A new library, serving both the Freer and the Arthur M. Sackler Gallery, is on the second level of the Sackler Gallery. (Before the Sackler opens, in 1987, the library remains in the Freer.) The library houses nearly 35,000 volumes, about half of them in Chinese or Japanese, and maintains subscriptions to more than 100 periodicals. More than 8,000 photographs and 50,000 slides may be examined in a special study facility. Hours: 10 a.m. to 5 p.m. Monday through Friday.

AT A GLANCE

One of the finest collections of **Oriental art** in the world is to be found here. These magnificent holdings from Asia and the Near East share exhibit space in the Florentine Renaissance palace-style building with a major group of 19th- and early-20th-century American works. A highlight of these is the opulent **Peacock Room of James McNeill Whistler,** permanently installed here in all its splendor of oil color and gold on leather and wood.

Chinese bronze tiger of the 9th century B.C., Western Zhou dynasty.

THE FREER GALLERY OF ART

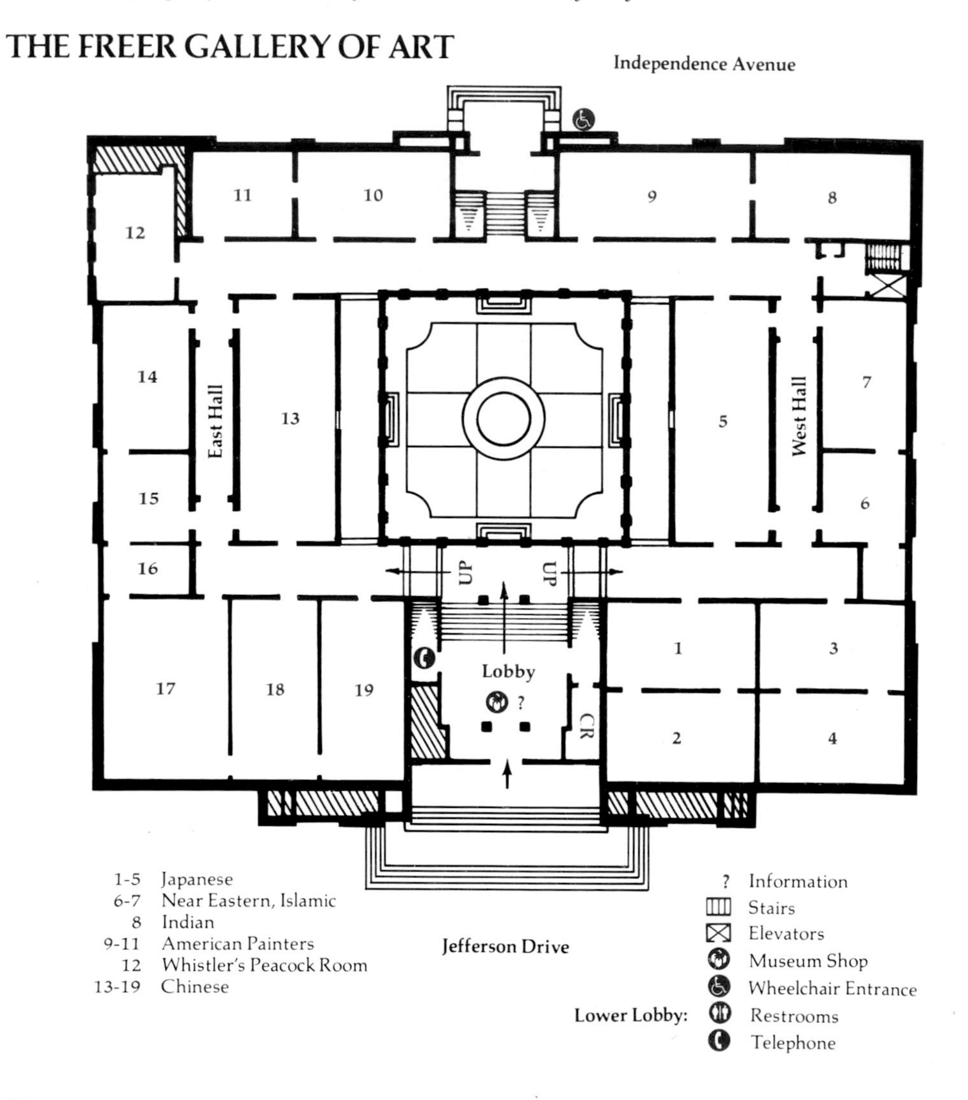

Chinese stoneware jar with carved decoration, Shang dynasty, late-13th–early 12th century B.C.

Chinese flask, early Ming dynasty, about 1400–1430. Porcelain with underglaze blue decoration.

The Freer Gallery of Art opened to the public in 1923, a gift to the nation from Charles Lang Freer, a Detroit businessman who combined an interest in Oriental art with American art of his time. He was a close friend of Whistler, upon whose advice Freer turned his attention to Asian art. At the same time that Freer was collecting art of the Orient, he was also acquiring American paintings whose subject matter and general tone and refinement he perceived as complementing his Oriental holdings, providing a bridge by which Westerners could reach an understanding of Eastern art.

Freer's deed of gift included both funds to construct a museum and an endowment for the study and care of the collection. His will stipulated that no works were to be added to the American collection after his death (he died in 1919), and it specifically forbade loans from, or to, any of the collections. The endowment income was to be used to add objects of the highest quality to the Oriental collection and carry on research in the civilizations of the countries in Asia in which the objects were produced.

As a result, the Freer collection of Asian art has been continuously and importantly augmented over the years. In close collaboration with the University of Michigan, the Freer also trains graduate students majoring in Oriental art. Scholars from universities and museums in all parts of the world regularly come to study and work here.

The Freer offers a schedule of changing exhibitions that reflect various aspects of the permanent collection, because only a fraction of the museum's more than 26,000 cataloged works of art can be displayed at any one time.

Japanese wall screen, Moonlight Revelry at the Dozō Sagami, *by Kitagawa Utamarō, 1754–1806. Edo period, 18th–19th century. Ink and color on paper.*

The Collections

Asian Art
China: bronzes, paintings, sculpture in stone and bronze, pottery and porcelain, jade, lacquer.
Japan: paintings, sculpture in wood and bronze, pottery and porcelain, works in metal and lacquer.
Korea: paintings, pottery, bronzes.
India: paintings, sculpture, pottery, metalwork, manuscripts.
Iran: paintings, sculpture, pottery, metalwork, manuscripts.
Egypt and Syria: sculpture, glass, pottery, manuscripts.
Also in the collections are Greek, Aramaic, and Armenian biblical manuscripts; and, from the Early Christian period, paintings, gold, and silver.

American Art
Foremost among the American artists represented in the Freer collections is James McNeill Whistler; indeed, the collection of his paintings, drawings, and prints is one of the largest in the world. His Peacock Room, executed in 1876/77 for a British merchant, is one of the gallery's most striking displays.

Other American works include paintings by Brush, Dewing, Hassam, Homer, Melchers, Metcalf, Murphy, Platt, Ryder, Sargent, Smith, Thayer, Tryon, and Twachtman; and sculptures by Saint-Gaudens.

Syrian canteen in brass, inlaid with silver, dating from the mid-13th century.

The Peacock Room, painted in 1876/77 by James McNeill Whistler for a British merchant. Oil color and gold on wood, leather, and canvas.

Chinese dish, Yuan dynasty, 14th century. Porcelain with underglaze blue decoration.

Shah Tahmasp Reading, *attributed to Aga Mirak, Iran, Tabriz, about 1530. Opaque watercolor on paper.*

ARTHUR M. SACKLER GALLERY

(Opening in 1987)

1050 Independence Avenue, SW
Open every day of the year except December 25, 10 a.m. to 5:30 p.m.
Telephone: (202) 357-2700

Entrance Pavilion Visitors enter the Sackler Gallery from Independence Avenue by way of a ground-level pavilion and then proceed by staircase or elevator to exhibition areas on two lower levels.
Information Desk In the entrance pavilion.
Tours Free guided tours are given daily at specific times. Special group tours must be scheduled at least two weeks in advance. Call (202) 357 3200 or 357-2104.
Museum Shop Books, posters, jewelry, cards, and gifts are for sale on the first level.
Library A new library, serving both the Sackler and the Freer Gallery of Art, is on the second level of the Sackler Gallery. (Before the building opens, in 1987, the library remains in the Freer.) The library houses nearly 35,000 volumes, about half of them in Chinese or Japanese, and maintains subscriptions to more than 100 periodicals. More than 8,000 photographs and 50,000 slides may be examined in a special study facility. Hours: 10 a.m. to 5 p.m. Monday through Friday.

AT A GLANCE

Visitors to the Smithsonian's newest museum—housed in an innovative below-ground building entered via a beige-granite and glass pavilion—may trace the development of Asian and Near Eastern art from ancient times to the present. A lively schedule of international exhibitions and interpretive programs complements the permanent collection.

Lotus, hanging scroll, China. By Qi Baishi (1863–1957). Ink and color on paper.

Bronze ritual vessel, "you," China. Shang dynasty, 13th century B.C.

The Arthur M. Sackler Gallery presents the artistic achievements of Asia and the Near East from 3,000 B.C. through the 20th century, spanning cultures from Japan to the Mediterranean.

Exhibitions include surveys of distinctive traditions in Asian art and also comparative presentations showing the work of different centuries and geographical areas as well as different types of patronage. For the first time at the Smithsonian, major gallery space is provided for the display of loan exhibitions of Asian art from important collections in the United States and abroad.

The Gallery's permanent collection is founded on a group of 1,000 art objects given by Arthur M. Sackler of New York City, a medical researcher, publisher, and art collector.

Octagonal box with Qiangjin decoration, China. Yuan dynasty, 1279–1368. Red and black lacquer and gold on wood.

Among Dr. Sackler's donations is a significant group of hanging scrolls by important 20th-century Chinese painters—the first major grouping of recent art from China in the Smithsonian's collections. In addition, there are Chinese bronzes spanning two millennia, jades from neolithic times to the present, paintings from the 10th century to the 20th, along with a variety of lacquer objects. Representing the Near East are sculpture and gold and silver objects from pre-Islamic times. The Sackler gift also contains an important group of bronze and stone sculpture from South and Southeast Asia.

An unparalleled set of Islamic and Persian paintings and manuscripts that had long been lost to scholars is included in the Gallery's growing collection. Uncovered through the sleuthing efforts of Smithsonian curators and purchased with special acquisitions funds, this collection embraces examples of almost all of the great classical Persian texts as well as several important Arabic works.

In addition to donating his collections, Dr. Sackler made a significant contribution to the construction of the museum and is also supporting a major program of scholarship and publication.

The Sackler Gallery shares its curatorial and educational facilities with the Freer Gallery of Art. The collections of these two museums, while separate, are complementary in period, style, and geographical origin—and thus offer unique opportunities for advanced research.

Carved lacquer tray, China. Southern Song dynasty, 1127–1279. Black, red, yellow lacquer on wood.

Jade and bronze dagger-axe, or "Ge," China. Shang dynasty, about 1200 B.C.

Bronze ritual vessel, "zun," China. Western Zhou dynasty, 10th century B.C.

Jade bear, China. Han dynasty, 1st century B.C.–A.D. 1st century.

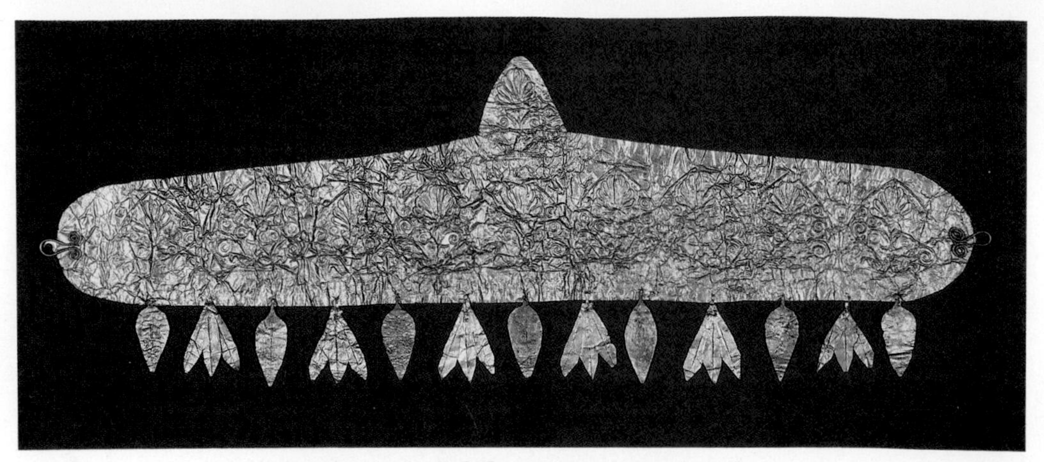

Gold hairband, Caucasus, 4th–3rd centuries B.C.(?)

Silver and gold-leaf rhyton, Iran (?), about 150 B.C.–A.D. 225

Adam and Eve Riding upon a Dragon and a Peacock, "Falnama" *manuscript, Iran, Tabriz, mid-16th century. Opaque watercolor on paper.*

This extraordinary figure, dated 1908, is a commemorative representation of an officer in the German colonial army who had cultivated a close relationship with King Njoya of Bamum, Cameroon Grasslands. Carved by a Fumban palace artist according to the king's specifications, the figure is the only free-standing life-size beaded figure known from Bamum. The crescent-shaped prestige cap, the brass facial sheath, the gesture of deference and the jewelry are symbols of status. (Gift of Evelyn A.J. Hall and John A. Friede)

NATIONAL MUSEUM OF AFRICAN ART

(Opening in 1987)

950 Independence Avenue, SW
Open every day of the year except December 25, 10 a.m. to 5:30 p.m.
Telephone: (202) 357-2700

Entrance Pavilion Visitors enter the National Museum of African Art from Independence Avenue by way of a ground-level pavilion and then proceed by staircase or elevator to the exhibition areas on two lower levels.
Information Desk In the entrance pavilion.
Tours Scheduled by appointment for adults and for secondary and elementary school groups. Call (202) 357-2700.
Museum Shop Books and exhibition catalogs, color reproductions, slides of art works, cards, posters, and a variety of unique gift objects are for sale.
Public Programs Workshops may be scheduled by appointment for adults and secondary and elementary school groups. Scholars are invited to lecture on aspects of current exhibitions and on topics in the field of African art. Outreach programs, conducted by staff and trained docents, tour the metropolitan region. Instructional materials for use by secondary school teachers are developed by the museum's Department of Education. These published

AT A GLANCE 

The arts and culture of sub-Saharan Africa are the focus of this museum, part of the Smithsonian's new Quadrangle complex. It is the only museum in the United States devoted to the exhibition, collection, and study of the visual arts of these diverse African cultures—some 900 in all—differing so markedly from Western traditions.

The figures of a woman and child created by a Zairian Yombe carver in the late 19th or early 20th century are prestige symbols of maternity, and as such may have had a connection with fertility rituals. This wood carving is one of six known Yombe maternity figures of that carving style—the only one in a public museum collection in the United States.

materials may relate to special exhibitions as well as to other, more general aspects of African art and culture. For information, call (202) 357-2700. TDD 357-1729.

Collections

Of the National Museum of African Art's present holdings of about 6,000 objects, some 2,000 works of sculpture were bequeathed as initial gifts by collectors Eliot Elisofon, Emil Arnold, and Samuel Rubin.

Among the more recent noteworthy acquisitions that enrich these holdings are a unique and well-documented sculpture of a life-size Bamum memorial grave figure, dated 1908, from the grassfields of Cameroon; an important example of Central African wood sculpture, a figure of a woman and child attributed to the Yombe people of Zaire; and a Yoruba (Nigeria) ivory female figure.

Exhibitions

Three to five major exhibitions a year are planned by the museum, along with a series of small, thematic ones. Included are exhibitions originated by the museum itself, often drawing on objects in the permanent collection, as well as exhibitions circulated by other museums.

Because the mandate of the National Museum of African Art is so clearly focused on sub-Saharan Africa, its exhibition program permits the presentation of the finest objects, allows for the examination of scholarly topics in depth, and encourages the development of experimental ideas. Exhibitions may be devoted to a single ethnic group or cultural region or they may be thematic in nature. Special interpretative audiovisual material, as well as lectures, film series, and workshops, may accompany the exhibitions.

Research

The Eliot Elisofon Photographic Archives—named for the famed *Life* magazine photographer—serves as a research and reference center of the museum. This archives consists of 150,000 color slides, 70,000 black and white negatives, about 50

This vessel with chameleons, about 1668–1773, is a tour-de-force of casting by the lost-wax method—a single cast piece. It is a creation of the Lower Niger Bronze Industry, which is characterized by a diverse grouping of object types and styles usually associated with Yoruba and Benin imagery.

feature films, and 100,000 feet of color motion picture film depicting traditional and contemporary arts and culture of Africa. It is a major and growing resource for academic institutions, museums, scholars, and the general public.

The collections of the Smithsonian Institution Libraries' National Museum of African Art branch, adjacent to the archives, complement these visual resources by providing reference and information services.

Both archives and library are open to the public by appointment only.

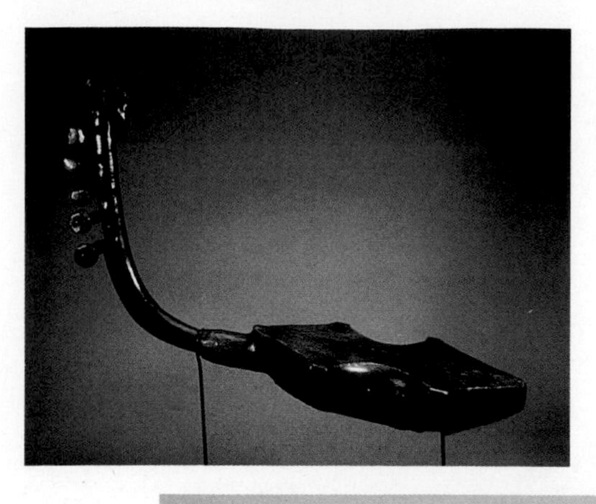

Favored by Zande notables, harps such as this one of wood, animal hide, and metal were renowned for their beautifully carved heads that were part of the dramatically curving necks separately attached to hour-glass-shaped sound boxes.

Dating from the early period of Benin, Nigeria, court art (1350–1550), this head is an outstanding example of the Benin bronze-caster's skill. With its marks of authority and relatively naturalistic appearance, the head is smaller than life-size and depicts either a Benin ruler or a defeated chief. Such commemorative heads were traditionally placed on ancestral altars.

The seated female figure of wood, cowrie shells, and rope (Senufo people, Ivory Coast, 20th century) is probably a staff top. The staff itself is a trophy of the cooperative work unit of which the champion cultivator is the standard bearer. Such staffs are display sculptures that appear when cooperative members work in the fields and also during their funerals. (Bequest of Eliot Elisofon)

Staffs surmounted by cast brass sculpture, called sono, *were used by chiefs as emblems of their leadership and royal lineage. This* sono *finial (Fulani or Soninke, Guinea-Bissau), one of a dozen surviving examples, depicts a single horseman with a male attendant, preceded by a woman.*

A view of the rotunda in Arts and Industries, the Smithsonian's second oldest building, completed in 1881.

ARTS & INDUSTRIES BUILDING

Jefferson Drive at 9th Street, SW
Open every day in the year except December 25, 10 a.m. to 5:30 p.m.
Telephone: (202) 357-2700

Information Desk At the entrance to the rotunda.
Tours Docents in Victorian costume give tours of the exhibition throughout the year. For information, call (202) 357-1481; TDD 357-1563.
Museum Shop Cards, books, jewelry, and items of Victoriana are featured. There is also a Smithsonian Catalog desk here.

Discovery Theater A changing series of programs, including films and presentations by puppeteers, dancers, actors, mimes, and singers. Performances are Tuesday through Saturday; for show times, tickets, and reservations call (202) 357-1500. (The theater is dark during the summer months.)

AT A GLANCE

In this Victorian landmark building is one of the most extensive collections of **Victorian Americana** ever presented. **"1876: A Centennial Exhibition"** comprises thousands of objects displayed in the style of the great Philadelphia Centennial Exposition, from which many of the exhibits were acquired. The rotunda of the building, with its fountain surrounded by flowers and plants that are changed seasonally, is a magnificent spectacle.

This is a half-size cutaway model of the "Centennial boiler." Babcock & Wilcox Company.

ARTS AND INDUSTRIES BUILDING

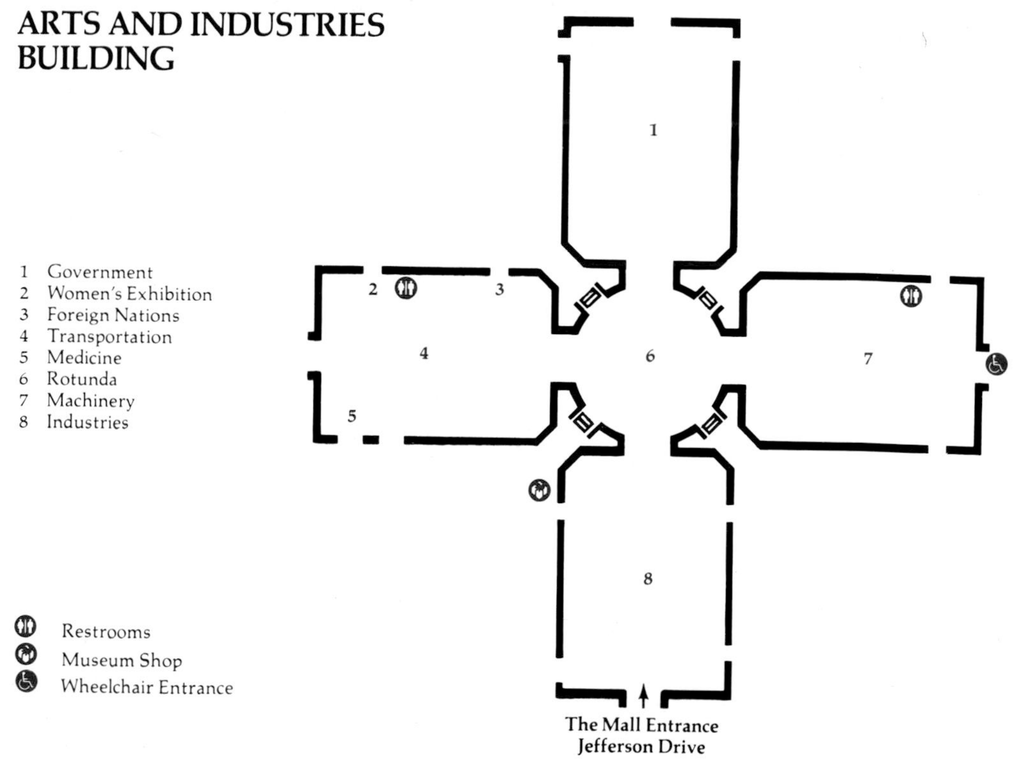

To step into the Arts and Industries Building, located just east of the Castle, is to step back in time—to the year 1876. That was the year of the grandest of all celebrations of America's centennial, the United States International Exposition, staged in Philadelphia. Known ever since simply as the Centennial, this exhibition marked the nation's coming of age. New wonders of technology were being perfected; the steam locomotive was conquering the land; the mysterious forces of electricity were being harnessed; and new methods of mass production were bringing to all segments of society some of the conveniences that previously had been reserved for the few.

The four main halls of the Arts and Industries Building are filled with objects that actually were shown at the Centennial or are of a design and appearance appropriate to that period. Here are steam-powered machines of every description—pumps, printing presses, machine tools, dynamos, and an awesome refrigeration compressor weighing more than 19 tons. Decorative touches include eagles, flowers, cupids, and other bits of Victorian whimsy. All sorts of manufactured goods are on display—from French lace to steel forgings, telescopes, a locomotive, silverware, perfume, and pistols. Not to be missed is the 45-foot-model of the naval cruiser *Antietam,* a steam sloop-of-war.

The Building

This exuberant structure of red brick and Ohio sandstone, with its colorful maze of roof angles, towers, and clerestories, was designed by Washington architect Adolph Cluss. The second oldest Smithsonian building on the Mall, known originally as the United States National Museum, it was built to house objects given to the Institution after the great Centennial Exposition closed in Philadelphia. The new building was completed in 1881, just in time for President James Garfield's Inaugural Ball in March of that year.

Over the years, the Arts and Industries Building (as it was renamed) housed a variety of collections, including aircraft, that have since been moved to newer Smithsonian museums. In 1976 the building was restored to its original appearance for the nation's Bicentennial celebration, and Centennial era exhibits were returned to its display halls.

The extensive restoration of the Arts and Industries Building was honored by the American Institute of Architects in 1980 for capturing "the essence of the original building without imitation of the past. . . . It is a real and lasting expression of Americana."

David Smith (1906–1965), Cubi XII, *1963.*

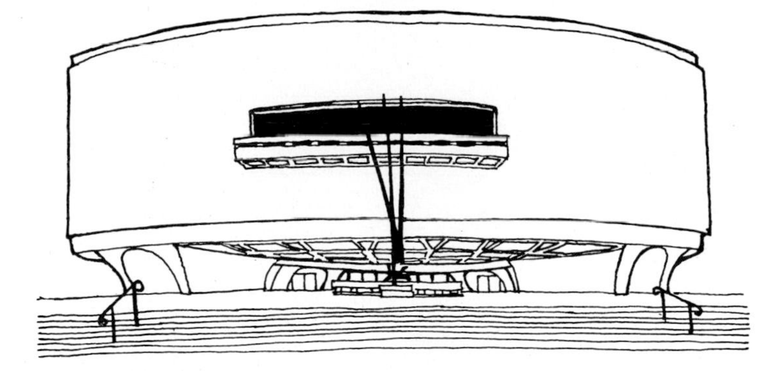

HIRSHHORN
MUSEUM & SCULPTURE GARDEN

Independence Avenue at 8th Street, SW
Open every day of the year except December 25, 10 a.m. to 5:30 p.m.
(Extended spring/summer hours determined annually)
Telephone: (202) 357-2700

Information Desk Located in the lobby.
Tours Guided walk-in tours are available Monday through Saturday at 10:30 a.m., 12 noon, and 1:30 p.m., and Sunday at 12:30 p.m., 1:30 p.m., and 2:30 p.m. In addition, general and specialized tours may be scheduled for school groups and organizations. Individual and group tours for the handicapped may also be arranged. At least two weeks' notice is required for these specially scheduled tours. Call (202) 357-3235.

Café A small, self-service café is operated outside the museum on the plaza, seven days a week from approximately mid-April to mid-September.
Museum Shop Located on the plaza level, the shop offers exhibition catalogs, slides, postcards, reproductions, books on art, and other items related to the museum's programs.
Special Events Free films and lectures are offered periodically in the auditorium on the lower level. For information, call (202) 357-2700.

AT A GLANCE

The emphasis here is on **European and American art from the late 19th century to the present day.** From **Cubism** to **Social Realism,** from **Abstract Expressionism** to **Pop, Op,** and **Minimal** art, this museum provides a **capsule course in the history of modern art.** The sculpture collection is exceptional, encompassing examples in a wide variety of materials by an impressive list of artists. Several major loan exhibitions—concentrating on a particular artist, theme, medium, style, or era—are mounted each year.

Auguste Rodin (1840–1917), The Burghers of Calais, *1886.*

Strollers Because of the damage strollers can cause to low-hanging paintings, they are not allowed in the galleries but must be left at the checkroom, where infant back-packs are available free of charge for use in the museum.

Constantin Brancusi (1876–1957), Torso of a Young Man, *1924.*

HIRSHHORN MUSEUM AND SCULPTURE GARDEN

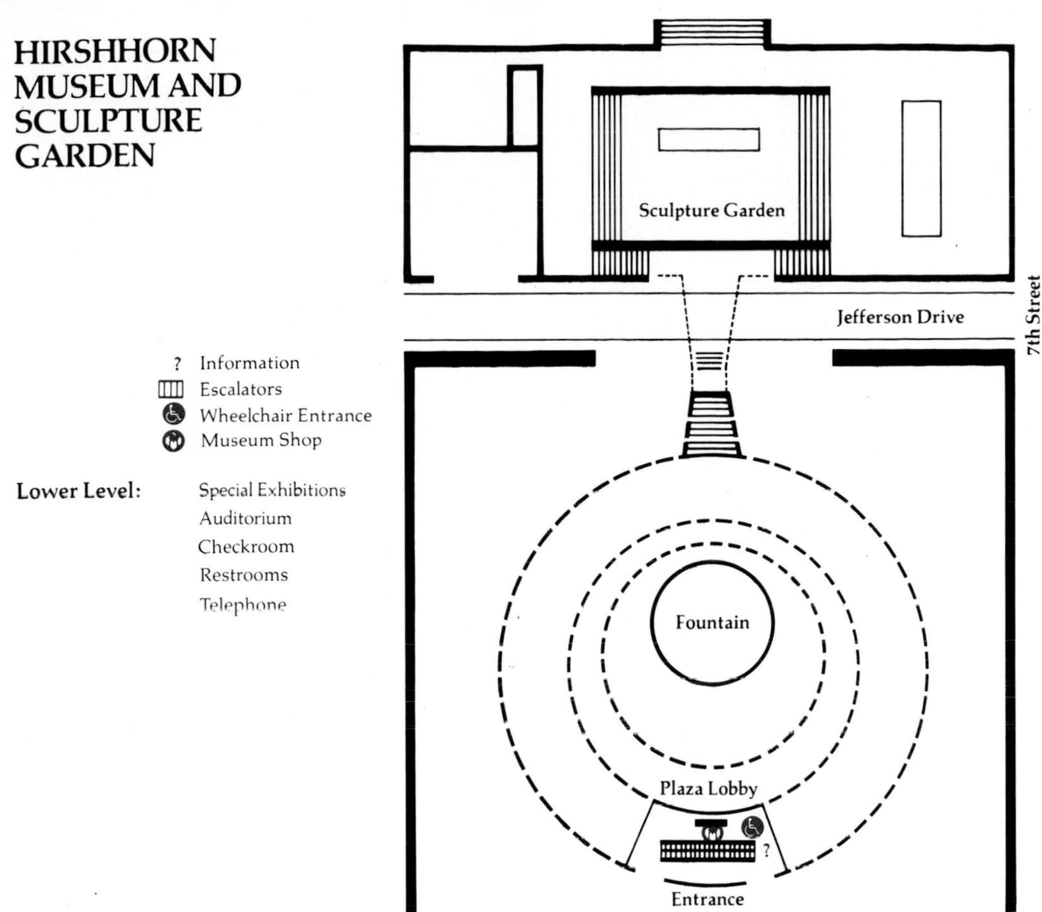

"If it were not controversial in almost every way, it would hardly qualify as a place to house contemporary art. For it must somehow be symbolic of the material it is designed to encase."

This description by former Smithsonian Secretary S. Dillon Ripley of the distinctive cylindrical building captures the Hirshhorn Museum and Sculpture Garden's essential character. Encased within its circular walls—and exhibited outside as well—is an impressive assemblage of works from a collection that holds some 5,000 paintings and 3,000 sculptures, as well as more than 4,500 works on paper. The nucleus of the collection, which provides a comprehensive view of major developments and trends in Western art from the late 19th century to the present, was donated to the people of the United States in 1966 by the dedicated and enthusiastic collector of art, Joseph H. Hirshhorn (1899–1981).

Works from the permanent collection on public display are rotated; thus what may be seen in any of the galleries at any given time will vary. In addition, important loan exhibitions may fill certain galleries at different times.

In general, sculpture is exhibited in the inner ambulatories of the second and third floors, which are naturally lighted by floor-to-ceiling windows; paintings and drawings are installed in the outer galleries, which are artificially illuminated to prevent light damage. By following the circular contours of the building, visitors can move easily from one gallery to the next. A large rectangular gallery generally used for special temporary exhibitions is on the lower level, along with the auditorium and

Morris Louis (1912–1962), Where, *1960.*

Alice Neel (1900–1984), Portrait of Sari Dienes, *1976.*

checkrooms. On the fourth floor are offices and a large study and storage area.

The Sculpture

The sculpture collection includes works in every medium by such European and American masters as Alexander Calder, Henri Matisse, Pablo Picasso, Auguste Rodin, and David Smith. In order to represent the development of 20th-century sculpture, the collection begins in the first part of the last century.

Among the precursors of modernism was Honoré Daumier, whose small, bronze caricature figures satirize the citizenry of the time of Louis Philippe. Another 19th-century artist represented extensively in the collection is Edgar Degas, whose small bronzes of ballerinas and women engaged in their daily tasks have the spontaneity of

Richard Estes (b. 1936), Diner, *1971.*

quick sketches.

Complementing such traditional forms of sculpture, the museum's collection also contains a broad range of modern works. Beginning with Constantin Brancusi's *Sleeping Muse,* the development of abstract sculpture can be traced to such present-day examples as Tony Smith's *Throwback* and Kenneth Snelson's 60-foot-high *Needle Tower.* Examples of contemporary sculpture include Joseph Cornell's intimate and mysterious boxes, Louise Nevelson's totemic wall pieces, Robert Arneson's witty ceramic busts, and Deborah Butterfield's scrap-metal horse.

The Paintings

While the sculpture collection offers a mix of American and European works, the painting collection is predominantly American. Again reaching back into the 19th century for precedents, such major American artists as Mary Cassatt, Thomas Eakins, and Winslow Homer are represented. The 20th century begins with the Ashcan School—those "radical" artists who chose to paint urban scenes. Artists of the Photo-Secession group—Arthur Dove, Marsden Hartley, John Marin, Alfred Maurer, and Georgia O'Keeffe—are also represented.

The collection is fortunate in having both early and mature examples of the work of the great Abstract Expressionist painters Willem de Kooning, Adolph Gottlieb, Franz Kline, Robert Motherwell, Jackson Pollock, and Mark Rothko. More recent painting is represented by artists as diverse as Frank Stella and Anselm Kiefer.

The collection of European painting,

though smaller, contains choice works by such 20th-century masters as Francis Bacon, Balthus, Fernand Léger, Joan Miró, and Piet Mondrian.

The depth of the collection presents some special opportunities. A number of important artists—Josef Albers, de Kooning, Henry Moore, and David Smith—are represented by such a large number of works that their entire careers can be traced. And many artists are represented by both paintings and sculptures. Among these are Arthur B. Davies, Jean Dubuffet, Max Ernst, Alberto Giacometti, and Matta.

The Building

Gordon Bunshaft's dynamic and unorthodox building—82 feet high and 231 feet in diameter—encircles an interior courtyard and an asymmetrically placed bronze fountain. The exterior wall is a solid surface, broken only by a 70-foot-long balcony and window on the third floor, overlooking the Mall. The open inner core has floor-to-ceiling windows overlooking the court. Four massive piers elevate the concrete structure 14 feet above the surrounding plaza.

All in all, the Hirshhorn is an instantly recognizable building—and an exciting showcase for the art within.

The Sculpture Garden

A number of monumental works of sculpture are strikingly exhibited both on the plaza surrounding the museum and in the Sculpture Garden itself. The sunken garden, with its rectangular reflecting pool, ranges from 6 to 14 feet below the level of the Mall and thus it provides a peaceful, quiet area for viewing art works.

Josef Albers (1888–1976), Homage to the Square Glow, *1966.*

Fernand Léger (1881–1955), Nude on a Red Background, *1927.*

Georgia O'Keeffe (1887–1986), Goat's Horn with Red, 1945.

The National Gallery of Art's East Building, a strikingly geometric contemporary structure by I.M. Pei, is linked to the original West Building by a paved plaza and an underground concourse with a moving walkway. In the East Building are exhibition galleries, the Center for Advanced Study in the Visual Arts, offices, library, photo archives, and service areas. In the central court hangs a huge Alexander Calder mobile.

The National Gallery of Art houses one of the finest collections in the world illustrating Western European and American achievements in painting, sculpture, and the graphic arts from the late Middle Ages to our own time.

Presenting the most comprehensive survey of Italian painting and sculpture in the Western Hemisphere, including the only painting by Leonardo da Vinci outside Europe, the collection is also particularly rich in the work of Rembrandt and the French Impressionists, and offers superb surveys of American, British, German, Flemish, and Spanish art as well.

The collection is on permanent display, and special international loan exhibitions are also presented in the gallery's two magnificent buildings.

Although formally established as a bureau of the Smithsonian Institution, the National Gallery of Art is an autonomous and separately administered organization governed by its own Board of Trustees. Free pamphlets describing the collections and services of the National Gallery are available in the buildings, or by writing to: National Gallery of Art, Washington, D.C. 20565

NATIONAL GALLERY OF ART

WEST BUILDING
Constitution Avenue at 6th Street, NW
Madison Drive at 6th Street, NW
EAST BUILDING
4th Street between Constitution Avenue and Madison Drive
Open every day of the year except December 25 and January 1
Hours: Weekdays—10 a.m. to 5 p.m. (9 p.m. April 1–Labor Day)
Sundays—noon to 9 p.m.
Telephone: (202) 737-4215

Information Desks At Constitution Avenue and Mall entrances to West Building; 4th Street entrance to East Building.
Tours An *Introductory Tour* is offered at 3 p.m., Monday–Saturday, and at 5 p.m. on Sunday. The *Tour of the Week* is at 1 p.m., Tuesday–Saturday, and at 2:30 p.m. on Sunday. The *Collection Highlight* gallery talk is at noon, Tuesday–Saturday, and at 2:00 p.m. on Sunday. *Recorded tours* may be rented for nominal fees. *Special tours* for groups of 15 or more can be arranged by applying at least two weeks in advance. Call (202) 842-6247.
Where to Eat A café and a cafeteria are located in the Concourse connecting the West and East Buildings; the Garden Café is in the West Building; the Terrace Café is in the East Building.
Sales Desks On the ground floor of the West Building near the Constitution Avenue entrance and in the Concourse.
Special Events Inquire at information desks about lectures, films, and concerts.

AT A GLANCE

A rich selection of works by **Old Masters** is to be found in this great art museum—Botticelli, Leonardo da Vinci, Raphael, Titian, Rembrandt, Rubens, and many others. Here, indeed, is the only painting by Leonardo in the Western Hemisphere. More recent masters are here, as well. In short, the gallery offers **one of the world's finest collections of European and American painting, sculpture, and graphic arts from the 13th century to the present.**

Albert Bierstadt (1830–1902), Among the Sierra Nevada Mountains, California.

Edward Hopper (1882–1967), Cape Cod Morning, *1950. (Gift of the Sara Roby Foundation)*

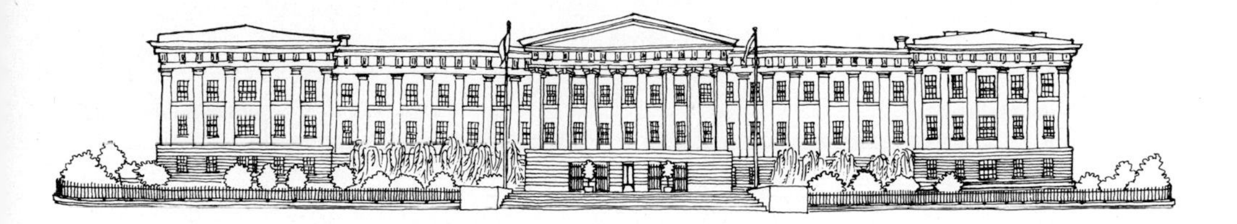

NATIONAL MUSEUM OF AMERICAN ART

8th and G Streets, NW (Metro Station: Gallery Place)
Open every day of the year except December 25, 10 a.m. to 5:30 p.m.
Telephone: (202) 357-2700

Information Desk Located at the G Street entrance.
Tours Guided walk-in tours are at noon Monday through Friday and at 1:45 p.m. on Sunday. Group sessions for children, high school students, and adults may be prearranged; guided Barney Studio House visits are available by appointment only on Wednesdays and Thursdays (except during the summer months). For reservations, call (202) 357-3111.
Special Events Free illustrated lectures and other public programs are offered periodically. For information, call (202) 357-3095.
Museum Shop Near the G Street entrance. On sale are museum publications and other art books, slides, reproductions, and postcards.
Where to Eat Sandwiches, salads, beverages, and desserts are available in a small first-floor café. The courtyard may be used for outdoor dining.
Prints and Drawings Study Room Open by appointment. Call (202) 357-2593.

AT A GLANCE

This museum, the oldest national art collection, presents 250 years of American painting, sculpture, photographs, and graphic art. Chronologically installed, the works of art begin with the colonial era on the ground floor and proceed upward to those of the modern era on the third floor. The historical sequence, however, is flexibly structured to allow for special groupings based on subjects, media, or other considerations. The magnificent Lincoln Gallery on the third floor was the site of Abraham Lincoln's 1865 inaugural reception.

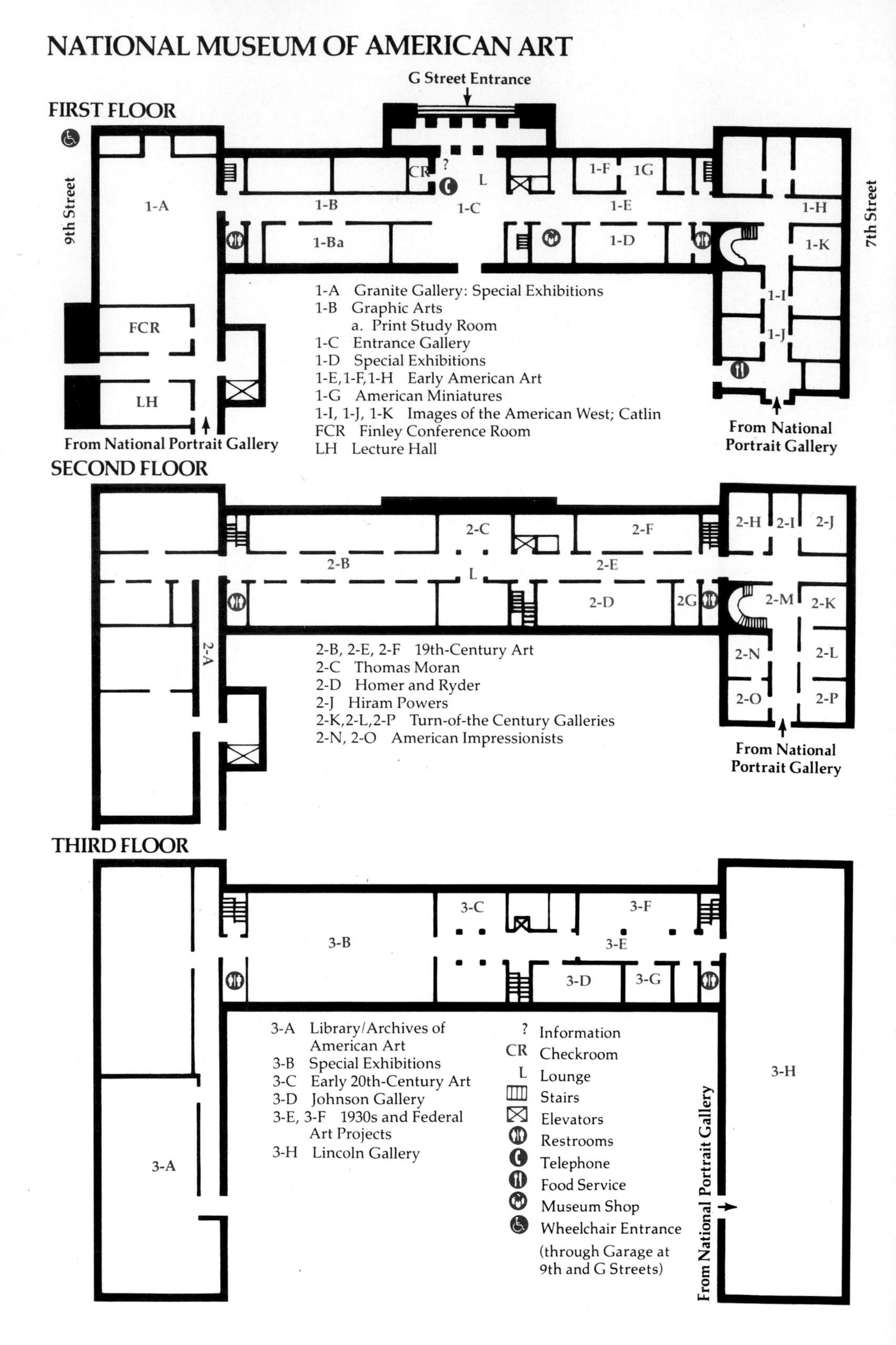
NATIONAL MUSEUM OF AMERICAN ART
G Street Entrance
FIRST FLOOR
9th Street
7th Street
1-A
1-B
1-Ba
CR
?
L
1-C
1-F
1G
1-E
1-D
1-H
1-K
1-I
1-J
FCR
LH
From National Portrait Gallery
From National Portrait Gallery
1-A Granite Gallery: Special Exhibitions
1-B Graphic Arts
a. Print Study Room
1-C Entrance Gallery
1-D Special Exhibitions
1-E, 1-F, 1-H Early American Art
1-G American Miniatures
1-I, 1-J, 1-K Images of the American West; Catlin
FCR Finley Conference Room
LH Lecture Hall
SECOND FLOOR
2-C
2-F
2-H
2-I
2-J
2-B
L
2-E
2-D
2G
2-M
2-K
2-A
2-N
2-L
2-O
2-P
From National Portrait Gallery
2-B, 2-E, 2-F 19th-Century Art
2-C Thomas Moran
2-D Homer and Ryder
2-J Hiram Powers
2-K, 2-L, 2-P Turn-of-the Century Galleries
2-N, 2-O American Impressionists
THIRD FLOOR
3-C
3-F
3-B
3-E
3-D
3-G
3-H
3-A
From National Portrait Gallery
3-A Library/Archives of American Art
3-B Special Exhibitions
3-C Early 20th-Century Art
3-D Johnson Gallery
3-E, 3-F 1930s and Federal Art Projects
3-H Lincoln Gallery
? Information
CR Checkroom
L Lounge
Stairs
Elevators
Restrooms
Telephone
Food Service
Museum Shop
Wheelchair Entrance (through Garage at 9th and G Streets)

Albert Pinkham Ryder (1847–1917), Moonlight.

Charles Willson Peale (1741–1827), miniature portrait of Matthias and Thomas Bordley.

Thomas Hart Benton (1889–1975), Achelous and Hercules, *1947. (Gift of Allied Stores Corporation and museum purchase through Major Acquisitions Fund, Smithsonian Institution.*

The National Museum of American Art presents a panorama of American painting, sculpture, graphic art, and photographs from the 18th century to the present. The more than 32,000 works in the collection range from 18th-century classical portraits through 19th-century sculpture, landscapes, and scenes of a developing land and its people, to the dynamic contemporary art of this century.

On permanent display in the galleries is a representative selection from the collection. Temporary exhibitions on various aspects of American art, accompanied by carefully researched publications, are shown regularly, and these frequently are circulated to museums and university galleries throughout the United States. All works not on display are available for study by visiting scholars.

As a major center for research in American art, the museum's resources include the Inventory of American Paintings Executed Before 1914, the Peter A. Juley & Son collection of 127,000 historic photographs, the Slide and Photographic Archives, the Smithsonian Art Index, the Pre-1877 Art Exhibition Catalogue Index, and the Joseph Cornell Study Center.

The library, shared with the National Portrait Gallery, contains 50,000 volumes on art, history, and biography, with special emphasis on the United States. It houses as well the Archives of American Art, with its vast holdings of documentary material on American art and artists.

Now part of the museum, the **Barney Studio House,** at 2306 Massachusetts Avenue, NW, was the second house on Sheridan Circle. It was built by Alice Pike

Barney in the first years of this century as a congenial setting for social and artistic events in emulation of Parisian salons. Mrs. Barney filled the house with her paintings and those of her friends—Edwin Scott, Edmund François Aman-Jean, Hubert Vos, and Charles Emile Auguste Carolus-Duran—as well as with carved furniture, Oriental rugs, and European decorative bibelots. Given to the Smithsonian in 1960 by Mrs. Barney's daughters, Natalie and Laura, the house has been carefully restored to evoke its original mood and intent as a place of artistic enjoyment.

The Collections

Both famous and lesser-known American artists are represented in the collections. Among the earlier artists are Albert Bierstadt, Asher B. Durand, Frederic E. Church, Ralph Earl, Winslow Homer, Thomas Moran, Charles Willson Peale, Thomas Cole, and Benjamin West. A large collection of miniature portrait paintings extends through 200 years of American art (galley 1-G, see floor plan), and 445 paintings of Indians by George Catlin are from the collection he showed in Paris in the 1840s.

The various trends in 20th-century painting and sculpture are represented by such artists as Franz Kline, Willem de Kooning, Romaine Brooks, Edward Hopper, William H. Johnson, Georgia O'Keeffe, Morris Louis, Robert Rauschenberg, and Paul Manship.

The lobby area—an introductory statement designed to show the diversity of the collection—juxtaposes paintings and sculpture ranging from classical to contemporary. It includes a major mural by Thomas Hart Benton as well as a recent acquisition that is changed monthly. Among the other works on the first floor (1-E, 1-F, 1-H) are landscapes, still lifes, and portraits from colonial days through the mid-19th century.

There also are galleries (1-I, 1-J, 1-K) devoted to images of the American West, with works by Frederic Remington, John Mix Stanley, and a selection of the George Catlin paintings. The Graphic Arts gallery (1-B) presents rotating exhibitions of prints and drawings from the permanent collection.

On the second floor are Hiram Powers's sculptures from his studio in Florence (2-J) and a large and choice group of Albert Pinkham Ryder and Winslow Homer paintings (2-D). Among the American Impressionists (2-N, 2-O) are Mary Cassatt, Childe Hassam, John H. Twachtman, and William Merritt Chase. In the lobby area (2-C) are three massive Thomas Moran paintings that represent the grand flowering of American landscape painting.

Also on the second floor (2-B, 2-E) are 19th-century paintings and sculpture by John Singer Sargent, Daniel Chester French, Augustus Saint-Gaudens, Frederic Edwin Church, and John Frederick Kensett. In the Turn-of-the-Century galleries (2-K, 2-L, 2-P) are paintings by Thomas Wilmer Dewing, Julian Alden Weir, John La Farge, and James McNeill Whistler.

The third floor is devoted to the 20th century, with two galleries (3-E, 3-F) featuring the works of the 1930s and the Federal Art Projects—the largest collection in the United States. Among the artists represented here are Charles Sheeler, Paul Cadmus, and Paul Manship. The Johnson Gallery (3-D) includes paintings and sculpture by early modernists such as Stuart Davis and John Sloan.

In the historic Lincoln Gallery (3-H) are works from the postwar era to the present—including those by Kenneth Noland, Morris Louis, Larry Rivers, Georgia O'Keeffe, Joseph Cornell, George Segal, Gene Davis, Milton Avery, Isamu Noguchi, Clyfford Still, and Robert Indiana.

History

The oldest national art collection in the United States, the National Museum of American Art moved into its first permanent home, the historic Old Patent Office Building, in May 1968. This was particularly appropriate because the beginnings of the collection, which predate the founding of the Smithsonian Institution, were exhibited in this same building as early as 1841.

Lincoln Gallery, National Museum of American Art. Left of pillar: Frank Stella's 1974 oil and lacquer on aluminum, maquette for Joatings I; *center: George W. Rickey's 1967–69 steel* Twenty-four Lines; *at rear: Jack Youngerman's 1961* July 26.

In 1829 a Washingtonian named John Varden began a collection he deemed fitting for the Nation's Capital. This collection—from which some works remain with the museum—was absorbed into the National Institute, which displayed its works of art beside those belonging to the government in the third-floor galleries of the then new Patent Office. Paintings and sculpture shared exhibition space with the original Declaration of Independence, shrunken heads, Benjamin Franklin's printing press, stuffed birds, and George Washington's commission as a commander of the Continental forces. In 1858 the collection belonging to the government was transferred to the Smithsonian Institution and, in 1862, the National Institute collection—including that of John Varden—followed.

In 1906 the collection was named the National Gallery of Art and it acquired paintings, sculpture, and memorabilia from Harriet Lane Johnston, the niece of President James Buchanan. No separate Smithsonian building was available and the expanding collection was allotted a hall in the National Museum of Natural History when it opened in 1909. As that became overcrowded, the works of art were either stored or lent to government offices throughout Washington.

Although the museum's history spans 150 years—including its designation as the National Gallery of Art until 1937 when that name was transferred to the Andrew Mellon collection—its works never had been properly shown until it moved into the Old Patent Office Building. From 1937 until 1980, the museum was known as the

Abbott Handerson Thayer (1849–1921), Angel, *1889. (Gift of John Gellatly)*

Romaine Brooks (1874–1970), Una, Lady Troubridge.

National Collection of Fine Arts. In October 1980, to reflect its decades-old policy of acquiring only American art, its name was changed by an act of Congress to the National Museum of American Art.

Many major gifts of paintings, prints, photographs, decorative arts, and sculpture have been added to the collection over the years, and today this magnificent edifice displays the wealth and variety of works created by American artists during the past 250 years.

Paul Manship (1885–1966), Flight of Europa, *1925. (Gift of Paul Manship)*

The courtyard of the Old Patent Office Building.

OLD PATENT OFFICE BUILDING

The historic Old Patent Office Building, halfway between the Capitol and the White House, now is shared by the National Museum of American Art, the National Portrait Gallery, and the Archives of American Art. An outstanding example of Greek Revival architecture, it is one of the finest structures of its kind in this country.

In 1836 Congress gave its approval for a "temple of the useful arts" to house the Patent Office and its models. During the Civil War, the First Rhode Island Militia was billeted here and, after the battles of Second Bull Run, Antietam, and Fredericksburg, 2,000 beds were placed on the marble floors for the casualties. Clara Barton, then a Patent Office copyist, helped care for the wounded, who were visited by Abraham Lincoln and Walt Whitman.

Five weeks before his assassination in 1865, President Lincoln held his second inaugural ball in the gas-lit building. Four thousand guests promenaded in what is now the Lincoln Gallery, a magnificent 264-foot hall with 32 marble pillars supporting a vaulted ceiling.

An attempt to raze this monumental building for a parking garage was thwarted in the mid-1950s. Congress decided, instead, to transfer it to the Smithsonian Institution.

John Singleton Copley (1738–1815), self portrait. (Gift of the Morris and Gwendolyn Cafritz Foundation with matching funds from the Smithsonian Institution.)

NATIONAL PORTRAIT GALLERY

8th and F Streets, NW (Metro Station: Gallery Place)
Open every day of the year except December 25, 10 a.m. to 5:30 p.m.
Telephone: (202) 357-2700

Information Desk Located at the main entrance (F Street).
Tours Guided tours are available on a walk-in or scheduled basis to individuals, school classes, families, the handicapped and other groups. Inquire at information desk; or arrange in advance by calling (202) 357-2920.
Museum Shop A Smithsonian gift shop specializes in history and art books and offers catalogs of exhibitions and the *Illustrated Checklist* of the National Portrait Gallery's permanent collection. Also for sale are such items as posters, jewelry, tote bags, and scarves.
Where to Eat A small café on the first floor serves lunch daily.
Special Activities and Research A wide variety of programs, materials, and services are available to schools and teachers, adult groups, and the general public through the Education Department. Call (202) 357-2920. The gallery also offers research services through other offices

From **Pocahontas** to **Jimmy Carter,** from **George Washington** to **Eleanor Roosevelt, Albert Einstein,** and **Robert Frost**—here are assembled more than 4,500 portraits of men and women who have contributed significantly to the history, development, and culture of the United States. Special exhibitions, the **Hall of Presidents,** and the *Time* magazine covers are among the displays not to be missed.

NATIONAL PORTRAIT GALLERY

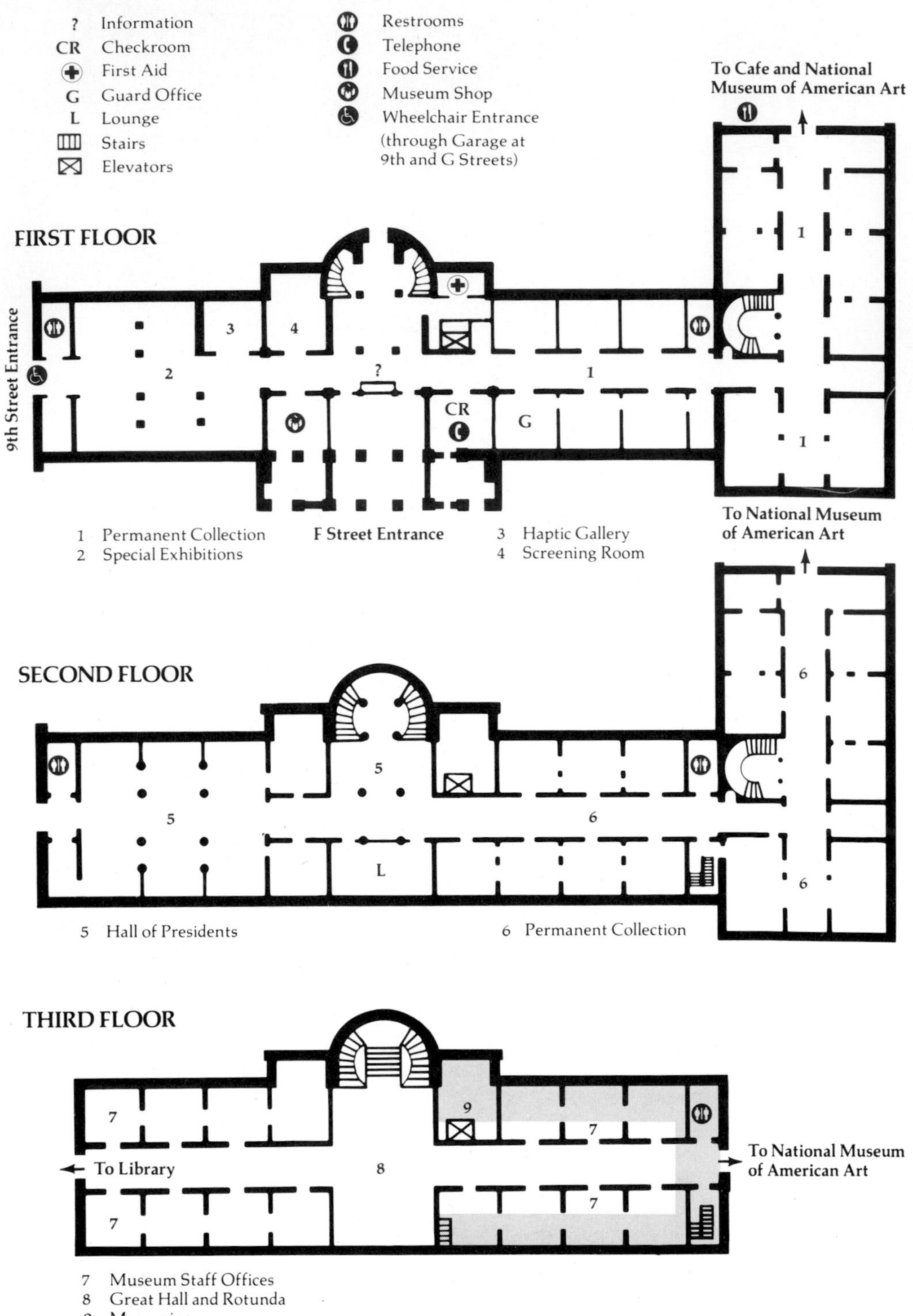

The Great Hall, third floor.

(access by appointment), including the Office of the Historian, the Catalog of American Portraits, and the library.

History and Objectives

A portrait, Thomas Carlyle believed, is "as a small lighted candle" by which biographies can "for the first time be read, and some human interpretation be made of them. . . . It has always struck me that Historical Portrait-Galleries . . . ought to exist . . . in every country, as among the most popular and cherished National Possessions."

The first official gesture toward creating a national portrait gallery in the United States was made in 1857 when Congress commissioned G. P. A. Healy to paint a series of presidential portraits for the

Abraham Lincoln (1809–1865), by John Henry Brown.

Isaac Merrit Singer (1811–1875), by Edward Harrison May. (Gift of the Singer Company.)

White House. In the decades following World War I, a national portrait gallery was seriously proposed as a part of the general art collection then developing within the Smithsonian Institution. The National Portrait Gallery of the United States was officially established by an Act of Congress in 1962, and opened to the public in 1968.

The gallery's holdings consist of paintings, sculptures, prints, drawings, and photographs, as directed by Congress, depicting "men and women who have made significant contributions to the history, development, and culture of the people of the United States." Since 1970 the collections have roughly quintupled in number and now approach 4,500 objects.

With the exceptions of Presidents of the United States, portraits are not admitted to the permanent collection or publicly displayed, except as part of a special exhibition, until 10 years after the subject's death. Under certain circumstances, however, the gallery may accept a portrait for later addition to the collection. The final decision on acquisitions rests with the National Portrait Gallery Commission. The gallery's preference is for likenesses taken directly from life, or for those that are at least contemporary with the subject. Nearly two-thirds of the portraits now in the permanent collection have come as gifts, and the rest were purchased with funds appropriated by Congress for the overall operation of the gallery.

Major loan exhibitions, as well as smaller shows, assembled from collections both in this country and abroad, highlight themes from American history or the art of portraiture. Fully illustrated catalogs accompany all major exhibitions. Through the gallery's Education Department, guided tours are available to individuals and groups.

The National Portrait Gallery is also a resource center for biography and portraiture, offering research services through several offices to which access may be arranged by appointment. Extensive biographical files are kept in the Office of the Historian. The Catalog of American Portraits, a unique reference facility, contains documentation, including photographs, on nearly 70,000 portraits of noted Americans, located in public and private collections throughout the country. The library, shared with the National Museum of American Art, contains 50,000 volumes, receives more than 800 serials, and houses an extensive collection of clippings and pamphlets on art subjects.

Gertrude Stein (1874–1946), by Jo Davidson. (Gift of Dr. Maury Leibovitz.)

The Exhibits

First Floor
Immediately to the right inside the main entrance (from F Street) is the information desk, the starting point for guided tours. Nearby is the Museum Shop. The museum's major temporary exhibitions are installed in the galleries to the left of the main entrance. In the corridor to the right of the entrance, selections of portrait prints and drawings from the permanent collection are displayed. The rooms off of this corridor contain special theme collections, such as portrait sculptures by Jo Davidson and the *Time* magazine cover portraits. A left turn at the far end of this corridor brings the visitor to the café.

Second Floor
The Hall of Presidents is at the west end, introduced by portraits of George Washington. The rest of the space is devoted to likenesses of notable Americans from the colonial period to the 20th century. In the second floor lounge is a collection of August Edouart portrait silhouettes.

Third Floor
Selections from the gallery's Civil War collection are displayed on the east mezzanine of the Great Hall.

This is the National Museum of American Art/ National Portrait Gallery Library, which is open to researchers by appointment.

Frederick Douglass (1817–1895), a portrait attributed to Elisha Hammond.

Henry David Thoreau (1817–1862), daguerreotype by Benjamin D. Maxham. (Anonymous donor.)

Mary Cassatt (1845–1926), oil on canvas by Edgar Degas, about 1880–1884.

The Grand Salon of the Renwick—handsomely furnished in the style of an opulent Victorian interior.

RENWICK GALLERY

Pennsylvania Avenue at 17th Street, NW
Metro Station: Farragut West (Farragut Square exit)
Open every day of the year except December 25, 10 a.m. to 5:30 p.m.
Telephone: (202) 357-2700

Information Desk Located at the entrance.
Tours Prearranged group tours for children, high school students, and adults may be arranged by calling (202) 357-2531.
Special Events Free films and illustrated lectures are offered periodically.
Museum Shop Located near the entrance. On sale are Renwick publications, other craft, design, and decorative art books, and craft objects relating to museum exhibitions.

AT A GLANCE

Changing exhibitions of **American design, crafts,** and **decorative arts**—both historic and contemporary—are featured in this architecturally magnificent building. The two principal rooms, the **Grand Salon** and the **Octagon Room,** are elegantly furnished in the opulent style of the 1860s and 1870s.

The Renwick Gallery, a curatorial department of the National Museum of American Art, opened in January 1972 as a National Showcase for American design, crafts, and decorative arts. Built during the Civil War period, it was the city's first art museum, the original Corcoran Gallery of Art. It was not until 1965, when the building was threatened with demolition, that it was transferred to the Smithsonian Institution, extensively renovated, and renamed for its architect, James Renwick. The gallery areas are devoted to temporary exhibitions and to a selection of crafts and decorative arts from the permanent collection.

The Grand Salon and the Octagon Room are among the handsomest interiors in Washington. The Grand Salon exemplifies the splendor of a sumptuous Victorian salon of the 1860s and 1870s. Except for a few works from the present Corcoran collection, the paintings are from the permanent collection of the National Museum of American Art. When the Grand Salon, then known as the Main Picture Gallery, first opened to the public in 1874, 115 paintings hung in tiers "according to no artistic classification." Natural light streamed in from the skylight during the day and, at night, 285 gas jets provided illumination.

The Octagon Room was designed for the crowning object of the Corcoran collection, the celebrated Hiram Powers female nude, *The Greek Slave.* At first, the graceful statue raised prudish Victorian eyebrows, but eventually the attitude of the public changed. The sculpture is now on view in the Corcoran Gallery of Art and the original plaster model is in the National Museum of American Art, as is a group of works from Powers's Florence studio.

The Building

The building itself is a major artistic achievement and its restoration is, in part, a result of the effort to preserve the character of the Lafayette Park-Pennsylvania Avenue area near the White House.

Assisted by his partner, Robert T. Auchmutz, Renwick specifically planned the building to house the private art collection of the wealthy Washington merchant and banker, William Wilson Corcoran. Construction began in 1858 but the Civil War intervened; from 1861 to 1869, the building was a warehouse for the storage of records and uniforms, and the headquarters of the quartermaster general.

Although the interior was not completed until 1874, a gala public preview was held in February 1871 with President and Mrs. Ulysses S. Grant presiding over a grand ball to raise additional funds for the Washington Monument.

Corcoran's collection of bronzes, paintings, and plaster replicas of famous statues occupied the building from 1874 until 1897, when the collections were moved to the new Corcoran Gallery of Art nearby. The United States Court of Claims took possession of the building in 1899 and used it for the next 65 years.

This handsome structure is a notable example of what today is known as the French Second Empire style. Corcoran's monogram and profile portrait appear with the motto, "Dedicated to Art," over the front entrance.

Lattice Physalia, *latticini glass, by Stephen Dee Edwards, 1982. (Gift of Steven Aarons, Barbara Aarons Fineblum, and Charles Fineblum in memory of their uncle, Harry B. Cohen) ©1982 Stephen Dee Edwards.*

Gates by Albert Paley, 1974. Forged mild steel, brass, and bronze; installed in the Renwick Gallery in 1976.

These marionettes were carved by William Buckner, Jr., while he was a student at M Street High School (now Dunbar) in Washington, D.C., 1903–1907. Anna Cooper, 1884 Oberlin graduate and one of the first black women to earn a four-year "gentlemen's degree," was the principal of the high school at that time. She has been the subject of a major exhibition at the Anacostia Neighborhood Museum.

One of the Smithsonian's off-the-Mall museums, the Anacostia Neighborhood Museum was founded in a community of the same name in southeast Washington, D.C. Its exhibitions focus on the Afro-American experience in the United States.

Among its major exhibitions have been: "The Renaissance: Black Arts of the Twenties"; "Black Women: Achievements Against the Odds"; "Black Wings"; "Blacks in the Westward Movement"; and "The Frederick Douglass Years: 1817–1895." Many of these and other exhibitions have been circulated nationally by the Smithsonian Institution Traveling Exhibition Service.

In developing its exhibitions and educational programs, the Anacostia Museum experiments with new techniques and formats. Because young people are a large part of the audience here, participatory programs encourage them to explore their notions of what a museum is. In addition, educational programs are designed to explain exhibition themes and to enlarge on related ideas.

Special activities for children visiting the museum include mini-exhibits and black history lessons featuring flannel-board stories, puppet shows, and guided tours.

After 20 years at its original location on Martin Luther King, Jr. Avenue, the Anacostia Neighborhood Museum moves into a new building in nearby Fort Stanton Park in March 1987—a 6,800-square-foot annex to the building that has long housed the exhibits laboratory, research department, and administrative offices.

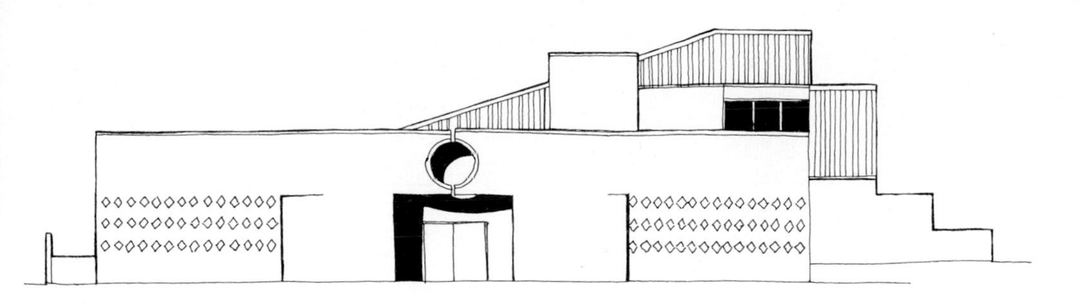

ANACOSTIA NEIGHBORHOOD MUSEUM

(New building opens March 1987)

1901 Fort Place, SE
Open every day of the year except December 25, 10 a.m. to 5 p.m.
Telephone: (202) 287-3369

How to Get There *By Metrobus:* Route B4. For information, call Metro at (202) 637-7000. *By car:* Take the Southeast Freeway (395) over the 11th Street Bridge to Martin Luther King, Jr. Avenue; at the third traffic light, make a left onto Morris Road and proceed about 10 blocks to the museum. Or take 295 to Howard Road; at the first traffic light, make a left onto Martin Luther King, Jr. Avenue, and at the next light, a left onto Morris Road. Ample parking is available for cars and buses.

Tours Call ahead to schedule tours, (202) 287-3369.

Special Events A Calendar of Events may be requested by writing to or calling the museum. For special scheduling call the tour information number, or write to the above address, Attention: Education Department (ZIP 20020).

Research Department Assistance is offered to graduate students and scholars in the field of Afro-American and ethnic studies, by appointment. Write to 1901 Fort Place, SE, Washington, D.C. 20020, or call (202) 287-3380.

AT A GLANCE

This unique museum was established in 1967 to stimulate Smithsonian participation in the intellectual contributions of a southeast Washington community composed predominantly of black citizens. Initially created as a "**neighborhood museum," with major focus on the history and cultural interests of the Anacostia community, the museum has broadened its coverage over the years and today reaches a national audience** via traveling exhibitions, educational programs, and publications.

One of the most elegant examples from the Cooper-Hewitt's extensive wallpaper collection is "The Peacock Garden," designed by Walter Crane in England, about 1889. Items from the museum's holdings in many design categories are shown from time to time in changing exhibitions covering a wide range of topics.

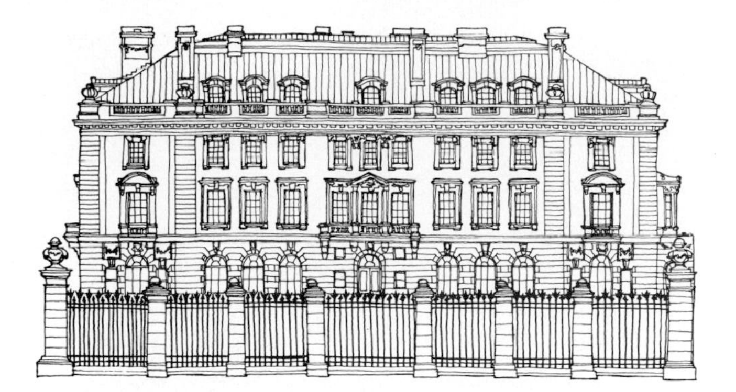

COOPER-HEWITT MUSEUM

2 East 91st Street (Fifth Avenue at 91st Street) New York, New York
Hours: Tuesday, 10 a.m. to 9 p.m.; Wednesday through Saturday, 10 a.m. to 5 p.m.;
Sunday, noon to 5 p.m. Closed Monday and major holidays
(Christmas, New Year's Day, Memorial Day, Fourth of July, Labor Day, Thanksgiving)
Telephone: (212) 860-6868

Information Desk Located just inside the main entrance.
Tours Guided tours are available for groups of six or more by arrangement in advance with the Programs office. This includes school classes, senior citizens, handicapped persons, and other groups.
Museum Shop Located near the main entrance, the museum shop offers exhibition catalogs; posters; slides; postcards; books on the decorative arts and architecture; books relating to the museum's collections and current exhibitions; and gift items of glass, porcelain, silver, and other materials—some of which are reproductions of collection objects.
Special Events The museum has an active program of workshops, courses, lectures, study tours, films, and seminars throughout the year. Performing arts include free concerts and dance programs. Weekend classes for young people are offered in handcrafts and elementary design.
Research Facilities Study facilities avail-

AT A GLANCE

The Smithsonian's national museum of design has **impressive collections of decorative art, furniture, work in precious and common metals, glass, woodwork, embroidery, woven and printed textiles, lace, and wallpaper.** It also has the largest collection of drawings in the United States, a large collection of prints, and an important library on the decorative arts.

Design for the music room's south wall, Royal Pavilion, Brighton. Frederick Crace, England, 1779–1859.

able by appointment include a library containing more than 40,000 books, many of them rare volumes, and a picture collection of almost one million items consisting of material related to color, pattern, textiles, symbols, advertising, and interior and industrial design.

Ceramic dog. Emile Gallé, 1870–80. Glazed earthenware, with polychrome decoration, and glass.

Founded by the granddaughters—Sarah, Eleanor, and Amy Hewitt—of New York manufacturer and philanthropist Peter Cooper, the Cooper Union Museum for the Arts of Decoration opened in 1897 and has continued to serve as a center for the study of design. Threatened with discontinuance because of the financial problems of its parent institution (Cooper Union for the Advancement of Science and Art), the museum was saved through a major fund-raising drive by its supporters and was transferred to the Smithsonian in 1968.

The name was changed to acknowledge its founders and heritage, and arrangements were made to move to the Carnegie Mansion, a Fifth Avenue landmark since it was built by Andrew Carnegie in 1901 at a cost of a million and a half dollars. In 1972 the property was given to the Smithsonian by the Carnegie Corporation. The renovation of the 64-room Georgian Revival mansion was done with a sensitivity both to its landmark status and to its function as an active public museum, permitting the dynamic display of objects, as well as the processes by which they are created, and the ways in which design affects our lives.

Since reopening to the public in its renovated building in 1976, the museum has had a continuing program of changing and diverse exhibitions drawn from its own and other collections. Although no part of the Cooper-Hewitt's permanent collection is on long-term view, collection objects are often selected from the museum's vast holdings for a current exhibition if they are pertinent to that show. In addition, the Cooper-Hewitt is a "working museum," serving as a reference center for designers, researchers, scholars, and students.

The Collections

Of enormous scope and diversity, the collections consist of design and decorative arts objects spanning most of the world's cultures over 3,000 years—although the greatest emphasis is on Western cultures of approximately the past 400 years. Major areas of collecting are drawings, prints, textiles, wallpaper, metalwork, woodwork, ceramics, and furniture. These collections are particularly strong in 17th-century through mid-19th-century examples, and the present direction is to expand with acquisitions of work of the late 19th and 20th centuries, including examples of contemporary urban and industrial design.

The museum's collections were assembled with a singular purpose: to provide visual information for the study of design. As a result, they have a remarkable cohesion. The objects in the collections are divided in terms of medium and technique rather than culture, period, or historical chronology, and primary consideration has been given to providing a ready cross-reference among the collections and with the library.

Giant pandas Ling-Ling and Hsing-Hsing came to the United States in 1972 as gifts from China.

NATIONAL ZOO

AND SMITHSONIAN BIOPARK

Entrances: Connecticut Avenue, NW (3000 block between Cathedral Avenue and Devonshire Street); Harvard Street and Adams Mill Road intersection; Beach Drive in Rock Creek Park

Open every day of the year except December 25

Hours: GATES—Open at 8 a.m.

Entrance gates close when buildings close; exit gates close at 6 p.m. during winter months; 8 p.m. in warmer months

ANIMAL BUILDINGS—Open at 9 a.m. Close at 4:30 p.m. during winter months; 6 p.m. in warmer months

Telephone: (202) 673-4800—information recording; (202) 673-4717—information desk

Public Transportation The Woodley Park/ Zoo subway station is conveniently located. Some Metro buses also serve the Zoo. For Metro information, call (202) 637-7000.

Parking Limited, pay parking is available on Zoo lots. Provisions are made for bus passenger discharge, pickup, and free bus parking.

Food and Picnic Facilities A variety of fast food facilities are available. Picnic areas are located throughout the grounds, but no outdoor cooking is permitted.

Visiting Groups and Tours No advance arrangements are necessary for visiting groups. Guided school group tours, provided by volunteers of the Friends of the National Zoo, are available from October through May by advance reservation. Call (202) 673-4955.

Pandas from China, kiwis (flightless birds) from New Zealand, golden lion tamarins from Brazil, and invertebrates from around the world are just a few of the animals at the National Zoo. Each year millions of visitors come to this attractive and extensive park to see these and others of the approximately 2,500 animals of nearly 500 species on exhibit in naturalistic settings.

Caribbean flamingos are among the more than 180 types of birds on display in the park.

Services Ramped building entrances and rest room facilities are available for nonambulatory visitors. Strollers may be rented in season for a small fee. Zoo Police and Health Units provide first aid, lost and found service, and a refuge for lost children.
Gift Shops Unusual zoo-oriented articles—souvenirs, postcards, books, T-shirts, art objects—are offered for sale.
Panda Feeding Times About 11 a.m. and 3 p.m. Giant pandas are most active at feeding time. The times other animals are fed vary considerably, according to the season and the keeper work schedule. The big cats and the bears are not fed in exhibit areas.
Helpful Hints Consider using Metro; Zoo parking lots often fill up early. Wear comfortable clothing and shoes. Don't overexert in hot weather—find a comfortable

This pink-tipped sea anemone is one of the many species of invertebrates to be seen at the Zoo.

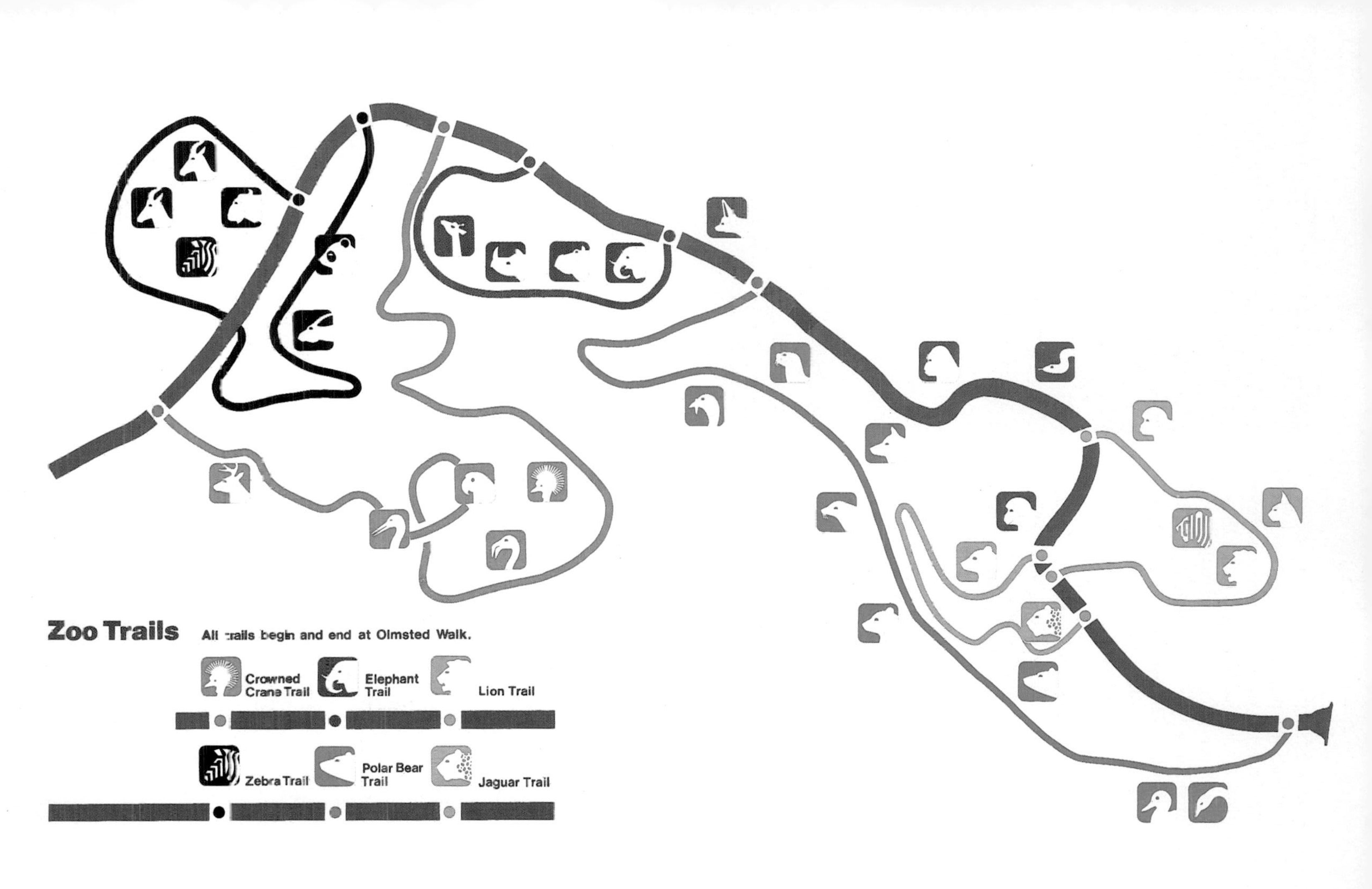
Zoo Trails
All trails begin and end at Olmsted Walk.
Crowned Crane Trail
Elephant Trail
Lion Trail
Zebra Trail
Polar Bear Trail
Jaguar Trail

pace. Take advantage of the films at the Education Building. Plan to visit early in the day or in the evening (during warmer months)—the crowds are gone and the animals are more active. Fall and early winter are great times to visit the Zoo.

Some Rules to Follow, Please:

Pets are not permitted in the Park. Dogs and other pets frighten Zoo animals and may spread disease.

Stay on your side of the guard rail. Zoo animals are wild and easily excited. The area between the guard rail and the enclosure barrier is provided for your safety and the safety of the animals.

Please do not feed the animals. The Zoo provides its animals with excellent balanced diets; additional feeding is unhealthy for them.

Golden lion tamarins became an endangered species in their native Brazil as development destroyed parts of their unique forest home. This is one of a large colony of the colorful little monkeys bred at the National Zoo.

The National Zoo and Smithsonian Biopark is world famous for the display, breeding, and study of wild animals. Visitors can view most of the animals in naturalistic settings where social groups that approximate those found in the wild are comfortably housed.

The 163-acre biological park is set in the picturesque and sharply cut stream valley of Rock Creek at the fall line from the Piedmont plateau to the Atlantic coastal plain. Steep, wooded hillsides form backdrops for many of the animal exhibits, and a variety of native as well as ornamental plants add to the beauty of the Zoo's landscape. Pleasing architectural variety and styles of animal displays are apparent among the 16 major animal exhibit complexes on the Zoo grounds. Olmsted Walk—the Park's central walkway, where all the animal trails begin and end—is named for the renowned landscape architect, Frederick Law Olmsted, who prepared the original design for the National Zoo.

Of course, the 2,500 animals are the focus of attention at the Zoo. A fine variety of vertebrate species, representative of the most spectacular forms of land animals, make up the largest portion of the collection. Invertebrate and aquatic species, as well as biological communities, have been added in recent years to provide a more comprehensive picture of animal life for Zoo visitors. Educational graphics and learning labs enrich public understanding of the Park's animals and plants.

Among the Zoo's prominent features is a house for the great apes. Especially designed for gorillas and orangutans, this building has dry-moat-enclosed outdoor animal yards and indoor exhibit spaces equipped with climbing structures two stories high.

Elsewhere in the Zoo is a series of natural-appearing outdoor enclosures known as Beaver Valley, situated along a beautifully landscaped walkway. Living there are numbers of active mammals, including seals, sea lions, otters, beavers, and wolves.

Its large size and versatile trunk help make the Asiatic elephant a popular exhibit animal.

An Indian rhinoceros, born in 1974 at the National Zoo, was the first of this seriously endangered species to be born and raised in North America.

Totems with information panels mark the beginning and end of animal theme trails.

A thoughtfully organized sample of invertebrate life—a broad classification including insects, sponges, sea stars, worms, mollusks, crabs, and numerous other animals without backbones or spinal columns—may be viewed at the Invertebrate Hall, located behind the Reptile House. The National Zoo's reptile and amphibian programs and displays are considered among the best in the world. In the Small Mammal House, more than 50 species of animals live in naturalistic settings. And in the Great Flight Cage, visitors walk among 30 species of the more than 180 types of birds on display in the Park.

The **Education/Administration Building** contains classrooms, an auditorium where zoo and wildlife films are shown, a bookstore, and a public educational facility called **ZOOlab** (open Tuesday-Sunday, noon to 3 p.m.).

Conservation and Research

There is a great deal more to the National Zoo than the animals on public exhibit. Behind the scenes, conservation and research programs are conducted in animal behavior, ecology, and propagation. At the animal hospital and scientific research building on the Zoo grounds and at the **Conservation and Research Center** in Front Royal, Virginia, zoologists are constantly working to learn more about wild animal ecology and behavior in order to improve the care of animals in captivity and facilitate their breeding. On the 3,150-acre tract in Virginia, particular emphasis is on long-range breeding programs for many rare species, with the participation of other zoos. In recent years, the National Zoo has also sponsored and taken part in ecological programs in many parts of the world—and these have contributed greatly to the knowledge of the biology and behavior of wild animals.

History

Almost from its beginnings, the Smithsonian Institution received gifts of live animals—but there was no zoo in Washington then and hardly any place to put them. Some were sent off to zoos elsewhere; some were kept on the Mall, and over the years, a sizable menagerie accumulated outside the Castle. Then in 1889 Congress established the National Zoological Park at the urging of Samuel Pierpont Langley, the third Secretary of the Smithsonian, and naturalist William T. Hornaday, who was particularly concerned with saving the American bison from extinction. Six bison were among the animals transferred from the Mall to the new National Zoo.

Animal collecting expeditions in the 1920s and 1930s, along with gifts from individuals and foreign governments, and exchanges with other zoos, have all contributed to the Zoo's population. As the nation's "official zoo," the National Zoological Park is host to many delegations from foreign countries and receives many donations of unusual animals.

FONZ (Friends of the National Zoo)

This is a nonprofit membership organization of families and individuals who take part in special Zoo programs and support the goals of the National Zoo in conservation, education, and research. FONZ members serve as Zoo guides, help in animal behavior studies, receive wildlife publications, and are invited to behind-the-scenes events. Proceeds from the concessions operated by FONZ are used to further education and research programs.

Zebras—and other hoofed animals—are exhibited in large, natural enclosures offering unobstructed views.

Visitors can watch lions roaming the terraced hillside of their all-weather outdoor exhibit.

ESPECIALLY FOR CHILDREN

All Smithsonian museums contain objects that may especially intrigue young visitors, depending on their ages and individual interests. Some of the exhibits and features that have proved their constant appeal are listed here.

On the Mall

Uncle Beazley (life-size model of Triceratops dinosaur near the National Museum of Natural History)
Carousel (seasonal—in front of the Arts and Industries Building)

National Air and Space Museum

Theater: Films made especially for a giant screen provide thrills. (There is a fee; inquire at information desks for show times.)
Planetarium Special effects and an advanced planetarium instrument are combined in fascinating solar system presentations. (There is a fee; inquire at information desks for show times.)
Popular Exhibits
Moon rock and Apollo 11 Command Module (Milestones of Flight)
Walk through Skylab (Space Hall)
Mechanized puppets (Balloons and Airships)
Simulated moon landing (Apollo to the Moon)
U.S.S. *Smithsonian* aircraft carrier (Sea-Air Operations)
Starship *Enterprise* (Rocketry and Space Flight)

National Museum of Natural History/ National Museum of Man

Discovery Room: A completely touchable exhibit area for natural-history specimens; docents are on duty. (Open Monday–Thursday: noon to 2:30 p.m. Friday, Saturday, and Sunday: 10:30 a.m. to 3:30 p.m.). Groups—more than five persons—admitted by written prearrangement only; call (202) 357-2747 for application form.
Insect Zoo: Live insects, arachnids, crustaceans, millipedes, and centipedes in simulated natural environments. An active beehive is included. Volunteers give demonstrations of Zoo inhabitants. Groups—more than five persons—admitted by prearrangement only; call (202) 357-2747.
Other Popular Exhibits
African bush elephant and Bengal tiger
Dinosaurs and Ice Age mammals
Blue whale and living coral reef
Indian, Eskimo, African, Asian, Pacific, and South American displays
Ode to the Pinniped, a film that tells about fin-footed seals, seal lions, walruses.

National Museum of American History

Demonstration Centers: Electricity and the Spirit of 1776 (everyday life of citizen-soldiers) explored in demonstrations and discussions led by docents. (Inquire at information desks for schedules.)
Demonstrations: Techniques and sounds from the past can be seen and heard in the halls of Power Machinery, Textiles, Graphic Arts. **"Hands on History Room"** (visitors can handle reproductions of 18th century objects).
(Inquire at information desks for schedules.)
Popular Exhibits
Early autos, racing cars, bicycles
Steam locomotive with soundtrack
Dolls' house
First Ladies' gowns

Arts and Industries Building

Discovery Theater: Changing programs, including presentations by mimes, puppeteers, dancers, actors, and singers. Performances Tuesday–Saturday; for show times, tickets, and reservations, call (202) 357-1500. Sponsored by the Resident Associate Program.

Youngsters can take part in activities at the Smithsonian Environmental Research Center south of Annapolis at Edgewater, Maryland. Many ecology programs are offered for children and family groups. For information, call 216-4190 in the Washington area or (301) 798-4424.

All eyes are on the stage during a performance in the Discovery Theater, Arts and Industries Building.

National Zoological Park

The giant pandas, the big cats, the great apes, the elephants, and the snakes continue to be Zoo favorites—with many of them in new quarters.

ZOOlab and HERPlab: Find out more about the animals by exploring, looking, touching, and reading. Visit ZOOlab in the Education/Administration Building and HERPlab in the Reptile House. (Tuesday–Sunday, noon to 3 p.m.)

BIRDlab: Visit BIRDlab when you visit the Bird House . . . look closely at eggs, feathers, nests . . . try on a wing. . . . find out what birds eat. (Open on an irregular schedule, usually weekends, noon to 3 p.m.)

Ask at Zoo information desks about other special activities.

A young visitor examines a crocodile head, one of the Discovery Room's many touchable specimens at the National Museum of Natural History.

THE SMITHSONIAN ASSOCIATES

Individuals and families can participate in many of the activities of the Smithsonian Institution by joining the Smithsonian Associates, a self-sustaining public education program. Membership in either the National or Resident category provides the following benefits:

Subscription to *Smithsonian*
This popular and colorfully illustrated monthly magazine of the arts, sciences, history, ecology, the environment—any and all subjects that interest the Smithsonian itself—draws extensively on the resources and facilities of the Institution. Published only for members, it is not available at newsstands or in bookstores. Although written for adults, *Smithsonian* appeals to younger readers as well.

Travel and Selected Studies Programs
Associates are eligible to take part in a variety of Domestic or Foreign Study Tours and Selected Studies Seminars led by Smithsonian staff members or visiting scholars. A list of travel opportunities and seminars can be found in *Smithsonian* magazine.

Associates' Reception Center and Lounge
Both the center and the lounge, a quiet Victorian hall, are located in the Castle, the original Smithsonian building. Upon arrival, members and their families can expect a cordial welcome and orientation to the Institution.

The Court
Members and their families may enjoy a moderately priced buffet in the private Associates' dining room on the first floor of the National Museum of Natural History. Operated seven days a week, this facility also serves breakfast on weekends, and provides additional meal service when museum hours are extended seasonally.

Discounts on Gifts
Members receive a 10 percent discount on all purchases made in the various Museum Shops (excluding the National Gallery of Art and the National Zoo).

Discounts on Books
Associates receive a discount on purchases of books published by the Smithsonian Institution Press. A catalog describing current publications will be sent on request. Associates also receive a discount on books from other publishers, sold through the Museum Shops and the Smithsonian Bookstore in the National Museum of American History.

In addition to membership benefits just described, Resident Associate members also receive:

- The *Smithsonian Associate,* a monthly newsletter describing lectures, seminars, films, and performances, as well as courses, workshops, tours, and activities for young people. Resident Associates, young and old, may participate at reduced rates; some activities are free.
- Subscription discounts for *The Wilson Quarterly* and *Air & Space* magazine.
- Further discounts on some activities for members 60 and over.
- Discounts on original works of art commissioned by the Resident Associate Program.
- Volunteer opportunities.

Other Smithsonian Membership Programs
The Smithsonian's self-sustaining membership programs also include: the **Contributing Membership** and the **James Smithson Society,** whose members receive all the benefits of the National and Resident Associate Programs plus invitations

to special gala receptions, exhibition previews, film premieres; complimentary publications, recordings, and exhibition catalogs; limited access to the Commons, the handsome dining room in the Castle, reserved for staff, special scholars, and Contributing Members; reduced-rate participation in Resident Associate programs; and for Smithson Society members, an invitation to the annual James Smithson Society Weekend, featuring special tours and programs and a formal dinner.

Air and Space Associate Membership provides benefits that include: *Air & Space* magazine; participation in special free lectures at the National Air and Space Museum; eligibility for National and Air and Space Associate seminars and Foreign and Domestic Study Tours; reduced rates for Langley Theater films and Einstein Planetarium presentations at the National Air and Space Museum; discounts on purchases from the Smithsonian's Museum Shops, the Institution's gift catalog, and the book and record divisions of the Smithsonian Institution Press.

Several other Smithsonian museums and facilities, such as the Cooper-Hewitt Museum in New York and the National Zoo in Washington, offer involvement opportunities and special benefits through their own membership programs.
For further information about Smithsonian membership programs, please contact the Visitor Information and Associates' Reception Center, Smithsonian Institution, Washington, D.C. Telephone: (202) 357-2700; TDD (202) 357-1729.

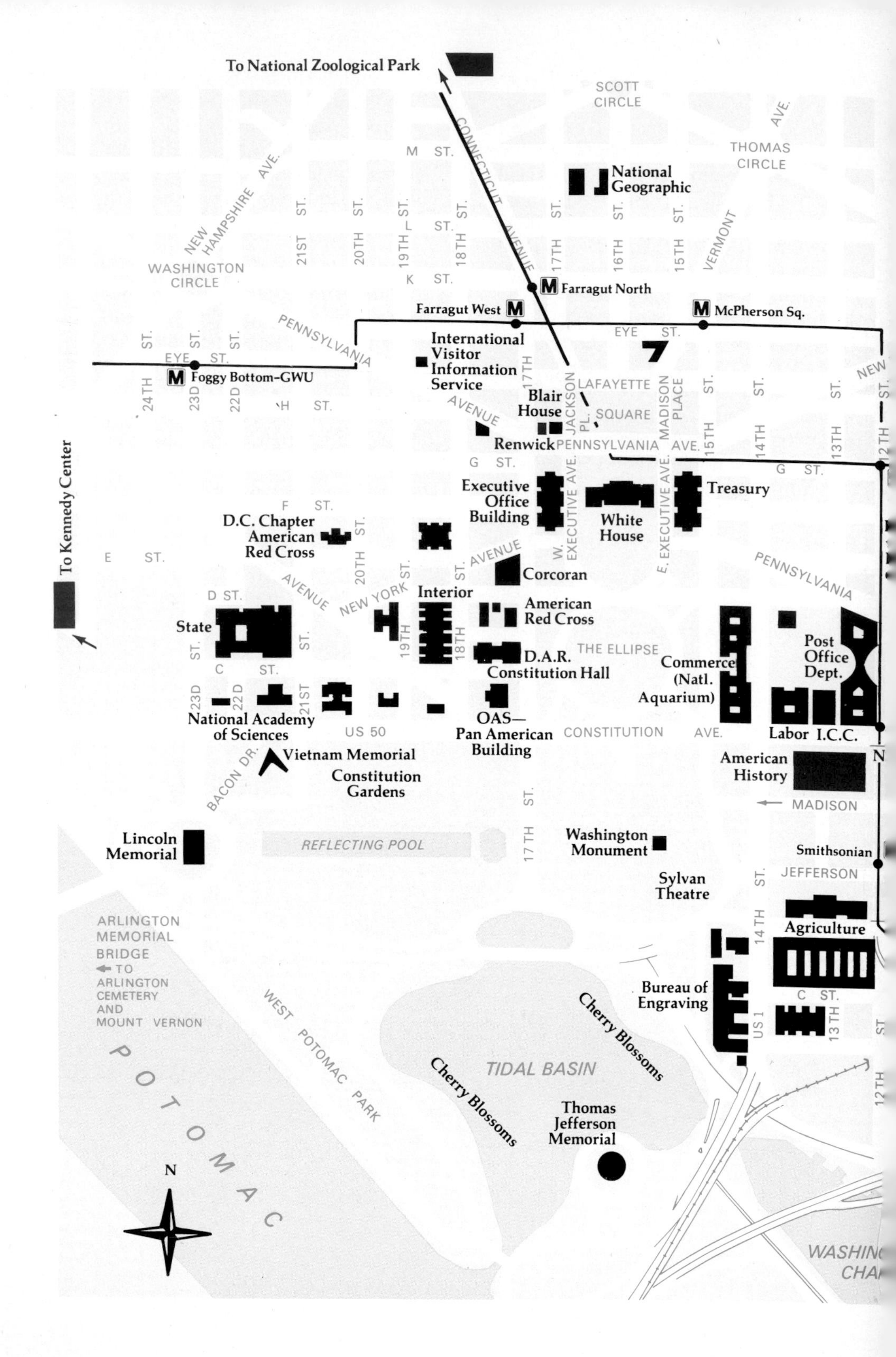

To National Zoological Park
SCOTT CIRCLE
THOMAS CIRCLE
National Geographic
WASHINGTON CIRCLE
NEW HAMPSHIRE AVE.
CONNECTICUT AVENUE
VERMONT AVE.
Farragut North
Farragut West
McPherson Sq.
Foggy Bottom-GWU
PENNSYLVANIA AVENUE
International Visitor Information Service
Blair House
LAFAYETTE SQUARE
JACKSON PL.
MADISON PLACE
Renwick
PENNSYLVANIA AVE.
Executive Office Building
White House
Treasury
W. EXECUTIVE AVE.
E. EXECUTIVE AVE.
To Kennedy Center
D.C. Chapter American Red Cross
Corcoran
Interior
NEW YORK AVENUE
American Red Cross
State
D.A.R. Constitution Hall
THE ELLIPSE
Commerce (Natl. Aquarium)
Post Office Dept.
National Academy of Sciences
OAS—Pan American Building
CONSTITUTION AVE.
Labor
I.C.C.
Vietnam Memorial
Constitution Gardens
American History
MADISON
BACON DR.
US 50
Lincoln Memorial
REFLECTING POOL
Washington Monument
Smithsonian
JEFFERSON
Sylvan Theatre
Agriculture
ARLINGTON MEMORIAL BRIDGE
TO ARLINGTON CEMETERY AND MOUNT VERNON
WEST POTOMAC PARK
Bureau of Engraving
Cherry Blossoms
TIDAL BASIN
Thomas Jefferson Memorial
POTOMAC
N
US 1

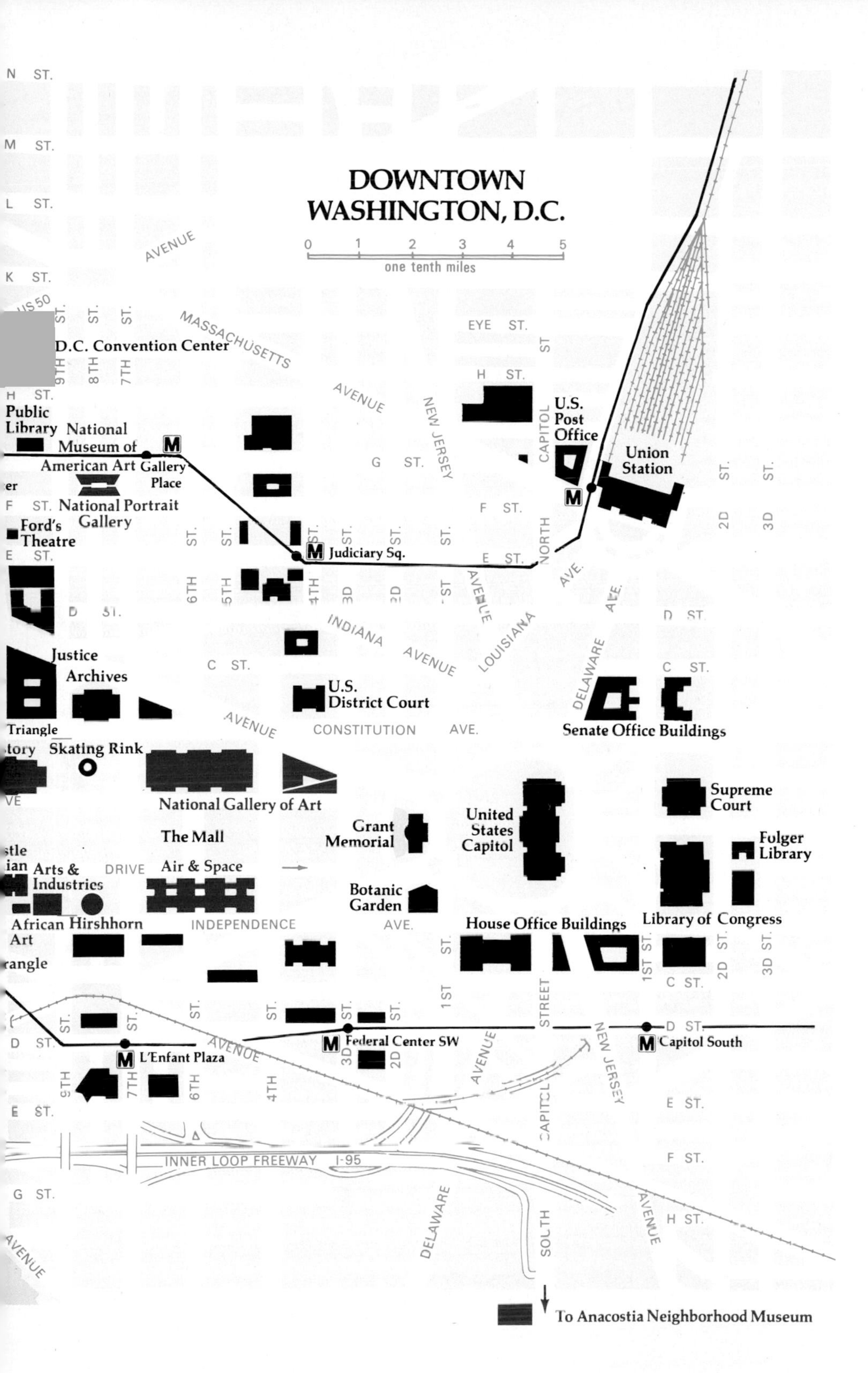
DOWNTOWN
WASHINGTON, D.C.
0 1 2 3 4 5
one tenth miles
N ST.
M ST.
L ST.
K ST.
H ST.
F ST.
E ST.
D ST.
C ST.
G ST.
EYE ST.
AVENUE
US 50
MASSACHUSETTS
AVENUE
NEW JERSEY
9TH ST.
8TH ST.
7TH ST.
6TH ST.
5TH ST.
4TH ST.
3D ST.
2D ST.
1ST ST.
NORTH CAPITOL ST
D.C. Convention Center
Public Library
National Museum of American Art
Gallery Place
National Portrait Gallery
Ford's Theatre
Judiciary Sq.
U.S. Post Office
Union Station
INDIANA AVENUE
LOUISIANA
DELAWARE AVE.
Justice
Archives
U.S. District Court
CONSTITUTION AVE.
Senate Office Buildings
Triangle
Skating Rink
National Gallery of Art
The Mall
Grant Memorial
United States Capitol
Supreme Court
Folger Library
Arts & Industries
DRIVE
Air & Space
Botanic Garden
African Art
Hirshhorn
INDEPENDENCE AVE.
House Office Buildings
Library of Congress
Federal Center SW
Capitol South
L'Enfant Plaza
INNER LOOP FREEWAY I-95
DELAWARE
SOUTH CAPITOL STREET
To Anacostia Neighborhood Museum

NOTES